RC
569.5
.V55
A84

Askenasy, Hans

Are we all Nazis?

7520003

8.95

D1499733

# ARE

# WE

# ALL

# NAZIS?

# ARE WE ALL NAZIS?

by

Hans Askenasy

Lyle Stuart Inc.    Secaucus, N.J.

Lee College Library
Baytown, Texas

*To the millions of men, women, and children*
*who did not live to tell it.*
*And whom you and I will join unless . . .*

First edition
Copyright © 1978 by Hans Askenasy
All rights reserved, including the right to reproduce
this book or any portion thereof in any form
Published by Lyle Stuart Inc.
120 Enterprise Ave., Secaucus, N.J. 07094
Published simultaneously in Canada by George J. McLeod Limited
73 Bathurst St., Toronto, Ont.
Address queries regarding rights and permissions
to Lyle Stuart Inc.
Manufactured in the United States of America

Library of Congress Cataloging in Publication Data

Askenasy, Hans, 1930—
Are we all Nazis?
Bibliography: p. 121
1. Violence. 2. Social psychiatry. 3. Homicide—Psychological aspects. 4. Sociology.
5. Holocaust, Jewish (1939–1945) I. Title.
RC69.5V55A84                301.6:33                77-13596
ISBN 0-8184-0248-2

# CONTENTS

## Acknowledgments

I am deeply grateful to Professors Albert Ellis, Gustave Gilbert, and Ellen Greenberger and to Nobel Laureate Gunnar Myrdal and Alva Myrdal for their comments and support; to Lyle Stuart, who asked me to rewrite the original manuscript in this simpler style, but never asked me to change a single thought; and to my daughter Thais for many reasons. May her world be a better one.

# Introduction

Do you really believe man's
conduct on earth could be considered sane by a rational person?

I WAS BORN ON MARCH 9, 1930, IN FRANKFURT AM MAIN, Germany, where my life almost ended on that day fifteen years later. A bomb fell on the last house still standing on the street but did not explode. Before the month was out Patton's Third Army had occupied what was left of the city.

And what was it like in the Germany of 1930? Form of government: the dying Weimar Republic. Religion: half Protestant, half Catholic. Jews constituted about 1 percent of the population. Social system: deformed. Economy: malfunctioning. Legacy of World War I: unresolved. If you were a typical German burgher you would long for some economic, social, and political stability; dislike the inefficient and supposedly democratic government; hate the former enemies of the war, and the thought of having lost it; be more or less anti- Semitic like almost everyone else; and be proud of being a "good" German: patriotic, industrious, efficient, military, and, above, all obedient.

And then there was Hitler, with whom you had to come to terms. You could actively oppose him; only a handful made this choice. But let it be remembered that the first to go to the gallows in Germany in 1933 were Germans. Or you could go on with life as usual. Many more did. (There has never been a shortage of people who just don't give a damn. Do you know how many tens of millions of eligible voters in the United States never voted in their entire life?) Or you could become an active Nazi. A large number chose that option. Why? Some did not know, or want to know, the real Hitler (nobody seemed to read *Mein Kampf*). A great many knew perfectly well but were so opportunistic that nothing else mattered. And some believed it all.

And what would you have done? Give it some thought, and take your time. For if you answer the question honestly—and don't be too sure you know if you do—you will begin to understand what this book is all about.

But I was not a typical German burgher: my father, a career jurist and city attorney, happened to have had

Jewish parents. Which made me "half–Jewish," whatever that may mean. And so it all began. In order to get a feeling for how it went, assume that *you* were a Jew in Nazi Germany. You can now empathize with Erica Jong when she writes in *Fear of Flying:*

> Sometimes, wandering around aimlessly, riding the Strassenbahn, shopping for beer and pretzels in a cafe, or *Kaffee und Kuchen* in a *Konditorei,* I would have the fantasy that I was the ghost of a Jew murdered in a concentration camp on the day I was born. Who was to tell me I was not?

Try to imagine the implications of the following to you; your wife or husband; your parents and your children; your friends and fellow humans:

| | |
|---|---|
| April 1933: | First official boycott of Jewish shops, lawyers, and doctors |
| September 1935: | Promulgation of the Nuremberg Laws for the "protection of German blood and honor" |
| August 1938: | Introduction of the compulsory additional middle names "Sarah" and "Israel" for all Jews |
| November 1938: | "Crystal Night" pogrom takes place throughout Germany. Destruction of synagogues, shops, and homes. At least 20,000 Jews imprisoned. Expulsion of all Jewish children from schools |
| September 1939: | Jews forbidden out of doors after 8:00 P.M. in winter and 9:00 P.M. in summer. Confiscation of all radios owned by Jews |
| September 1941: | Decree compelling Jews to wear a bright yellow star with the inscription *Jew* |

| | |
|---|---|
| January 1942: | The Wannsee conference, concerned with the "final solution of the Jewish problem" |
| June 1942: | Beginning of mass gassing at Auschwitz |

Some memories I have:

—standing in front of a Gestapo officer, his whip on the desk, and the tortured screaming in the cages in the cellar

—following an air raid, 286 bodies outside an "impregnable" fortified bunker which did not withstand a British blockbuster

—a Jewish acquaintance, a woman in her sixties, who turned on the gas of her stove in preference to "resettlement." She was ill and tired, and it was, no doubt, the logical thing to do

—my two older brothers working fourteen hours a day laying railroad tracks in a slave labor camp; my father, near death in a concentration camp in Czechoslovakia, liberated by Soviet troops

So we survived.

Almost six million Jews did not. Nor did the other millions of Nazi victims: the Russian civilians and prisoners of war; the gypsies and the homosexuals; the Polish intelligentsia and the mentally ill; the anti-Fascists everywhere.

On May 7, 1945, the Thousand Year Reich became history; it had lasted twelve.

At a quarter after seven in the evening of August 5, 1945, Washington time, an atomic bomb was exploded over a city named Hiroshima. Never were more humans killed in fewer seconds.

And nine days later the semi-divine emperor, in flowery language in an unprecedented radio address to his subjects, announced that "the war situation has developed not necessarily to Japan's advantage . . . " World War II was over.

And the ravaged earth was richer by sixty million corpses.

And what, if anything, was learned? Surely it could not all have been in vain? In fact nothing had, or has been, learned. The year the war ended another one began, in a largely unknown little country called Vietnam. It was to last three decades, cost millions of lives (as well as $150 billion), and see more bomb tonnage dropped than in all of World War II. It was also totally unjustified and totally unnecessary, and it ended in total defeat—the first in American history. A few said the obvious. General David Shoup, hero of the battle of Tarawa in 1943, holder of the Medal of Honor, Commandant of the United States Marine Corps, and President Kennedy's favorite service chief:

> From the beginning of our growing involvement in the affairs of Vietnam, I had opposed the idea that such a small country in that remote part of the world constituted either an economic interest or a strategic threat to the welfare of the United States. . . . There is considerable evidence that the National Liberation Front is in fact better organized and enjoys greater loyalty among the peoples of Vietnam than does the Saigon government. . . . We acquired a substantial degree of arrogance and assurance in our military power. Our thriving militarism deluded us into believing we had the means to solve most of the complex world problems that came within range of our guns and dollars. . . .[1]

And then came Algeria (and tortures committed by both sides) and Korea and Cuba; India and the Mideast; the Congo and the slaughter of the Hutus by the Watutsi; Lebanon and Angola. To be continued.

Only one thing is new: we become ever more efficient. And thus ever more dangerous. For mankind has so far survived due only to inefficiency. Consider what man has managed to do within the span of twenty-four hours. During the battle of the Somme in World War I British casualties were 60,000—on the first day. The crematories

---

[1]From his introduction to Colonel Donovan's *Militarism, USA* (1969).

at Auschwitz were designed to dispose of at least 7,000 bodies—a day. Man's expenditures on armaments in 1976 stood at $900 million—a day. And do you know how many people starve to death every day in this world? It is a very painful way to die.

And man can do, and will do, even better. There are now 1,710 American strategic missiles with 8,500 to 9,000 nuclear warheads and their 2,378 Soviet counterparts with 3,500 nuclear warheads pointing at each other. Which is to say, at those Russians and at us. And no one questions that most of them will get through. Which leads us to the Eichmannian Rand Corporation term *overkill*. Which even *sounds* insane.

The moral and mental defects of the human race and its leaders have thus been demonstrated with some exactitude. Yet the butchery goes on. And so, as expressed in the words of the cold-blooded Prussian general Alfred von Schlieffen: "It will happen as it has to happen."

Unless you and I find out what makes man behave so barbarically and idiotically—unless you and I decide to do something about it.

# 1.

# AUSCHWITZ, POLAND, 1943

"At that time, when the greatest number of Jews were exterminated in the gas chambers, an order was issued that the children were to be thrown into the crematory ovens or into the crematory ditches, without previous asphyxiation with gas . . . the children were thrown in alive. Their cries could be heard all over the camp."

Testimony at the *Trial of the Major War Criminals before the International Military Tribunal at Nuremberg,* 8:319.

THE REASON, IT TURNS OUT, WAS NOT EVEN SADISM: IT WAS simply cheaper that way.

Let us assume you and I had been arrested and were being sent to Auschwitz. Let me spare you the details of what it was like in the cattle cars in which Adolf Eichmann, who once described himself as a coordinator of railroad time tables, sent us there. This is where we were going.

In May 1940 a camp was set up at Oswiecim, a small town in Poland, 32 miles west of Cracow near the Czech border. Sometime later the adjacent town of Birkenau was converted into a barbed-wire enclosure large enough to hold 100,000 inmates. The two camps covered a 15-square-mile area, and were also known as Auschwitz I and Auschwitz II.

Convicted criminals were installed as the heads of the prisoner hierarchy, and the first inmates arrived in June 1940. By May and June 1942 the mass exterminations by gassing were under way.

> The two great crematoriums I and II were built in the Winter of 1942–1943, and put into use in the Spring of 1943. Each had five three-retort ovens, and each could cremate about 2,000 bodies in less than 24 hours. Technical reasons connected with keeping the fires going made it impossible to increase the capacity of the ovens. Attempts to do so resulted in serious damage, which on several occasions meant the complete breakdown of operations. . . . The two smaller crematoriums III and IV were capable, according to calculations made by the construction firm of Topf of Erfurt, of burning about 1,500 bodies within 24 hours. . . .

Thus wrote the commandant of Auschwitz.[1] And he continues:

> The killing itself took the least time. You could dispose of 2,000 head in a half hour, but it was the burning that took all the time. The killing was easy; you didn't even need guards to drive them into the chambers; they just went in expecting to take showers. . . . [2]

And then this:

> Through heavy-glass portholes the executioners could

watch what happened. The naked prisoners below would be looking up at the showers from which no water spouted or perhaps at the floor wondering why there were no drains. It took some moments for the gas to have much effect. But soon the inmates became aware that it was issuing from the perforations in the vents. It was then that they usually panicked, crowding away from the pipes and finally stampeding toward the huge metal door where . . . "they piled up in one blue clammy blood-splattered pyramid, clawing and mauling each other even in death."

Twenty or thirty minutes later when the huge mass of naked flesh had ceased to writhe, pumps drew out the poisonous air, the large door was opened and the men of the *Sonderkommando* took over. These were Jewish male inmates who were promised their lives and adequate food in return for performing the most ghastly job of all. (They were inevitably and regularly dispatched in the gas chambers and replaced by new teams who continued to meet the same fate. The SS wanted no survivors to tell tales.) Protected with gas masks and rubber boots and wielding hoses they went to work . . . : Their first task was to remove the blood and defecations before dragging the clawing dead apart with nooses and hooks, the prelude to the ghastly search for gold and the removal of teeth and hair which were regarded by the Germans as strategic materials. Then the journey by lift or railwagon to the furnaces, the mill that ground the clinker to fine ash, and the truck that scattered the ashes in the stream of the Sola.[3]

Cremation of the bodies also took place under the open sky, with human fat serving as supplementary fuel.

Life expectancy for those not selected for gassing immediately upon arrival varied between a few weeks and three months. Most victims were Jews.

The executions lasted until the end of October 1944. On November 27 the crematoria were blown up, and on January 17, 1945, the evacuation began in response to the advancing Red Army. Seven thousand sick prisioners were left behind. At 3:00 P.M. on January 27, 1688 days after the first transport of victims had arrived, Soviet reconnaisance troops of the First Ukrainian Front entered what had become the largest cemetery on earth.

SS Colonel Rudolf Hoess, the major commandant of Auschwitz, testified that at least 2.5 million victims were executed and exterminated there by gassing and burning, and at least another 500,000 succumbed to starvation and disease, making a total dead of about 3 million.[4] In his autobiography, written sometime later, he considers the number "far too high," stating that "even Auschwitz had its limits," and that he had obtained the estimate from Eichmann. A probable figure is around 2 million.[5]

So much for the camp. And then there were the guards. They all belonged to the SS, and a number of points concerning the Nazi elite should be made.

The SS, or *Schutzstaffel* ("Protective Formation"), wore black uniforms with caps adorned with an insignia in the form of a human skull; the implications should have been obvious. They began as a counterforce to the SA, or *Sturmabteilung* ("Storm Troop"), who wore brown uniforms, and broke the latter's power by executing the coup in 1934 which resulted in the murder of various SA leaders, including Ernst Roehm. (Roehm, the SA chief of staff in whom Hitler saw his rival, like so many others underestimated the Führer's ruthlessness. When arrested by Hitler himself he could only ask, "What's the matter, Adolf? Have you gone crazy?" A few weeks later two SS officers gunned him down in his cell.)

Of the more than a million men who eventually belonged to the SS, most served in the Waffen-SS, essentially its armed forces, which fought alongside the regular army as a sort of elite corps. Of them, 350,000 were killed in combat, testifying to their fanaticism and willingness for self-sacrifice. Some 50,000 SS men took part in the mass murders. One-third of those working for the extermination machinery were Austrians.

Heinz Hoehne, probably the most knowledgeable person about the SS and its members, concluded in *The*

*Order of the Death's Head: The Story of Hitler's SS* that it was never a monolithic organization, never a homogeneous group of men, but rather "a bizarre mixture of the idealist and the criminal, the ambitious and the romantic."

And this is what the SS did to the Jews (they had millions of other victims):

"THE FINAL SOLUTION"
Jews murdered in Germany and occupied countries[6]

| | |
|---|---:|
| Germany (including Austria and the Reichsprotectorate) | 290,000 |
| Slovakia | 75,000 |
| Denmark and Norway | less than 900 |
| Belgium, The Netherlands, and Luxemburg | 146,000 |
| France | 90,000 |
| Italy | 8,000 |
| Soviet Union (including Lithuania, Estonia, and Latvia) | 1,480,000 |
| Bulgaria | 14,000 |
| Poland | 3,000,000 |
| Yugoslavia | 26,000 |
| Greece | 54,000 |
| Rumania | 30,000 |
| Hungary | 450,000 |
| Total: | 5,933,900 |

So we continue our journey into the past, and as the train stopped at the unforgettable platforms at Auschwitz we were to meet our executioners. What were they like?

There were the small fry. Of the two thousand SS men stationed at Auschwitz between 1940 and 1945, twenty-two "intolerable cases" were tried by a West German court in Frankfurt. The trial lasted twenty months, from December 1963 until August 1965. Testimony revealed unspeakable atrocities committed by individuals against prisoners, though most of the killings were carried out routinely.

"The defendants exhibited aggressive and remorseless behavior, often laughing and smirking impertinently toward prosecution, witnesses, and the court," in the words of one observer. Foreign correspondents noted that those of the accused who still lived at home were by no means treated as outcasts by their communities.

Twenty of the twenty-two were convicted. All filed appeals. All were considered clinically normal.

The impact on public opinion was minimal. As one of the prosecutors commented shortly thereafter, "The majority of the German people do not want to conduct any more trials against the Nazi criminals."

Hans Hofmeyer, the presiding judge at the trial, remarked sardonically, "I have yet to meet anyone who did anything at Auschwitz."

And then there were the big wheels, the decision makers. And what were they like? But before we take a closer look at the four most important of them—Hoess, Eichmann, Heydrich, and Himmler—let us ask ourselves what we— you and I—would expect them to be like. What sort of man would say these things:

*Whether this mass extermination of the Jews was necessary or not was something on which I could not allow myself an opinion.* [Hoess]

*One hundred dead is a catastrophe. Five million dead is a statistic.* [Eichmann]

*[I shall be the first to take care of Hitler] in case the old man fucks up.* [Heydrich]

*We shall never be rough or heartless where it is not necessary, that is clear. We Germans, who are the only people who have a decent attitude toward animals, will also assume a decent attitude toward these human animals.* [Himmler]

What would we predict—that they are criminal? Abnormal: sadistic, psychotic, or insane? Different, at any rate, from you and me? But what if for some strange reason they aren't any of those things? What if the cold facts were to show that there, but for different circumstances, go you and I? What then?

Let us spend a few moments on these men and see.[7]

There was Rudolf Hoess, SS colonel and commandant of Auschwitz.

What sort of person do you think it takes to run man's most efficient and ruthless murder factory? What sort of attitudes, values, and standards of conduct might he have? What kind of father was he to his children? What could such a man possibly have to say for himself?

He was born in 1900 into a middle-class merchant family. His father was a devout Catholic who wanted his son to become a priest.

During World War I he passionately wanted to join the army. After the armistice, that wish led to his becoming a member of a *Freikorps* as a sort of nationalistic soldier of fortune. In 1922 he joined the Nazi party. After taking part in a political murder, he served five years in solitary confinement in, of all places, Dachau. In 1934 he enlisted in the SS. As first assignment, he was sent to Dachau, by now a concentration camp, for guard duty. He had married in 1929.

He was promoted to commandant of Auschwitz in June 1941, where he performed his "duties" for two and a half years.

Arrested after the war, he wrote his autobiography in a Polish prison. He was hanged in April 1947, at Auschwitz.

From his autobiography:

> From the beginning I was so absorbed, I might say obsessed, with my task that every fresh difficulty only increased my zeal. I was determined that nothing should get me down. My pride would not allow it. I lived only for my work.

> The process of selection, which took place on the unloading platforms, was itself rich in incident. . . . I remember . . . a woman who tried to throw her children out of the gas chamber, just as the door was closing. Weeping, she called out: "At least let my precious

children live." There were many such shattering scenes which affected all who witnessed them.

My family, to be sure, were well provided for in Auschwitz. Every wish that my wife or children expressed was granted them. The children could live a free and untrammeled life. My wife's garden was a paradise of flowers. . . .

I myself never maltreated a prisoner, far less killed one.

Unknowingly I was a cog in the wheel of the great extermination machine created by the Third Reich.

I also see now that the extermination of the Jews was fundamentally wrong . . . precisely because of these mass exterminations, Germany has drawn upon herself the hatred of the entire world. It has in no way served the cause of anti-Semitism, but on the contrary brought the Jews far closer to their ultimate objective.

So I face my sentence as a sacrifice of the system which I believed so fanatically. [8]

Let the public continue to regard me as the bloodthirsty beast, the cruel sadist, and the mass murderer; for the masses could never imagine the commandant of Auschwitz in any other light.

They could not understand that he, too, had a heart and that he was not evil.

The evidence indicates that, psychologically speaking, Hoess was essentially truthful in all these statements.

Professor Gilbert, the official United States psychologist at the Nuremberg Trial, interviewed and tested Hoess on numerous occasions. After one session Hoess said, "I suppose you want to know in this way if my thoughts and habits are normal."

Gilbert: "Well, what do you think?"

Hoess: "I am entirely normal. Even while I was doing this extermination work I led a normal family life, and so on."

Gilbert found that Hoess had superior basic intelligence, and characterized him as a "schizoid personality with a burnt-out superego." Concerning this diagnosis it should be noted that being schizoid (shy, withdrawn, having difficulties with interpersonal relationships) has no implications concerning either violence or ethical standards. *Superego* is not technically a clinical term, nor is it applicable in this context. As we have seen, Hoess had standards of conduct by which he abided. That is the whole point.

In summary, Hoess was an apathetic man, devoted to his family and fond of animals, schizoid but not psychotic, neither sadistic nor insane. He faithfully and fanatically believed in Nazi dogma, and in following orders, any orders, unquestioningly.

He was also the greatest mass murderer in human history.

And then there was SS Lieutenant Colonel Adolf Eichmann. Practically unknown even to Germans during the war, his trial in Israel was to make his name infamous throughout the world.

Karl Adolf Eichmann was born in 1906. His father, an engineer, was a deeply religious man; his mother died when he was four years old, and he was cared for by aunts. Later his family moved to Linz, Austria. He had some Jewish relatives and a Jewish girlfriend.

In 1931 he joined the Austrian Nazi party and then the SS. He was first assigned to an office dealing with "Zionist organizations" and thereafter to one dealing with Jewish emigration, which he strongly supported. Madagascar was mentioned as a possibility. Later he became a protégé of Heydrich, and in January 1940 he was put in charge of Gestapo Section IV-B-4. His assignment became the collection and deportation of Jews from all over occupied Europe to the extermination camps in Poland. He performed the task with extraordinary zeal.

Arrested by the Allies in March 1945, he escaped in November of the following year with the help of a Franciscan priest. Apprehended again by the Israeli security service in his hiding place in Argentina years later, he was surreptitiously flown to Israel.

In the dry official statement:

> The Israeli government asks the Argentine to take into consideration the significance of the fact that the man responsible for the assassination of millions of Jews has been brought before a court. In the event of a trespass upon Argentine law or on Argentine Sovereignty, the Israeli government expresses its regrets.

When tried in court, he pleaded "not guilty in the sense of the indictment" and was sentenced to death by hanging. Shortly before midnight on May 31, 1962, in Jerusalem, Israel, Adolf Eichmann met his final solution.

His body was cremated, and the ashes were scattered in the Mediterranean outside Israeli waters.

Simon Wiesenthal, the Viennese who has made it his life's task to find former Nazi criminals, played the major part in tracking down Eichmann. He had come to this conclusion:

> I had been wrong to look for a motive in his earlier life. There was no motive, no hatred. He was simply the perfect product of the system. . . . He would have done the same job if he had been ordered to kill all men whose name began with P or B, or all who had red hair.

The sociologist Hannah Arendt who covered his trial concurred:

> He was probably honest when he said . . . that he'd only done his job. He said he wouldn't have hesitated to send his own father into a gas chamber if he'd been ordered to do so.

And given his extraordinary efforts in continuing to send trainloads of victims to their extermination toward the end of the war, she said:

> The sad and very uncomfortable truth of the matter was that it was not his fanaticism but his very conscience that prompted [him] to adopt his uncompromising attitude.

And when Eichmann once stated that he was no anti-Semite, Wiesenthal agreed by adding, "But he was certainly anti- human."

In short, Eichmann was a minor organization man, a bureaucrat routinely executing his assignment. His defense attorney during his trial described his personality as that of a "common mailman." He was neither psychotic nor insane (half a dozen psychiatrists certified him to be normal), and there is no substantiated evidence that he was sadistic.

His name has become synonymous with the desk murderer.

There was Reinhard Heydrich, probably the most intelligent and formidable of all the Nazis.

He was born in March 1904 to Catholic parents. His father was a musician of some distinction. During the Weimar Republic he became a naval officer until he was expelled from the service for lying to a military court investigating a dubious love affair. The rumor that he was partly Jewish has not been substantiated.

Advancing quickly in the SS hierarchy, he became a general and, fully aware where the real power lay, chief of the *Reichssicherheitshauptamt* ("Reich Security Main Office"). As such, he was the immediate head of the Gestapo, the *Sicherheitsdienst* ("Security Service"), and the *Einsatzgruppen*, the mobile extermination units used in occupied territories to eliminate Jews and other "enemies."

On May 27, 1942, he was assassinated by a Czech commando when the Czech government in exile, for reasons of its own, felt the action to be called for. En route to the airport in Prague to fly to Berlin and see Hitler, he was engrossed in reading documents dealing with the extermination of undesirable Slavs when his open Mercedes slowed to round a curve. A grenade thrown into the car from a distance of twenty yards exploded, and lumps of wire, felt, leather, and glass lodged in his intestines. Mortally and painfully wounded, the "Protector of Bohemia and Moravia," as he was also officially known, died eight days later of blood poisoning. The first investigating police officer to see his death mask described it: "Deceptive features of unearthly spirituality and bottomless degenerate beauty, like a Renaissance cardinal.''

Following his death at least 1,300 Czechs were shot, and the town of Lidice was literally erased. Himmler, who feared Heydrich, was relieved. Another SS general, an old crony of Hitler and chief of his personal body guard, Sepp Dietrich, a former butcher, commented, ''Thank God the sow finally kicked the bucket.''

Reinhard Heydrich had superior intelligence and talent. He was an outstanding sportsman as well as a performer and patron of fine chamber music. As cited by Shlomo Aronson, his Israeli biographer, the chief of the Gestapo played ''tenderly and mellow, displaying first-class manners and an unquestioned sensitivity as violinist.''

He was dynamic, calculating, ruthlessly ambitious. He always had to be first, be it in fencing or in his performance in a whorehouse. He was given to sex and drink.

He had no ideological commitments. His ambition was power for its own sake. Consequently he did not detest Jews per se, and considered many of Himmler's ideas idiotic. According to Heinz Hoehne, ''Sadism at any rate did not constitute an essential part of his life.'' And Joachim C. Fest wrote in *The Face of the Third Reich:* ''Cunning was more in his line than brutality, and for an opponent to step unsuspectingly into an artistically constructed trap gave him a satisfaction he never derived from any aggressively brutal act.''

In sum, Heydrich was neither sadistic, psychotic, nor insane. He was a highly intelligent, talented, and ruthlessly opportunistic psychopath, the amoral technocrat passionately striving for power. At the time of his death he had become the most dangerous man in Nazi Germany, not excluding Hitler. His statement, quoted before, that he would ''take care'' of Hitler was no idle threat coming from a man of his power and cunning. There is little doubt that Frischauer in his book *Himmler* was right about Heydrich:

A hundred times when I discussed the Hitler regime with the most prominent survivors of the Nazi period, I have heard that sentence: "Had he lived he would have become Germany's Fuehrer sooner or later."

He was also one of the great criminal figures in history.

Finally, there was Himmler, the petty-bourgeois nonentity who was to become Europe's modern grand inquisitor. One of the earliest and most obedient followers of Hitler, he was rewarded by being put in charge of the entire SS empire. To give you the flavor of one side of Himmler:

> Whether the other people live in comfort or perish of hunger interest me only in so far as we need them as slaves for our culture . . . . Whether or not 10,000 Russian women collapse from exhaustion while digging a tank ditch interest me only in so far as the tank ditch is completed for Germany. It is a crime against our own blood to worry about them or assume that they are human as we are . . . . Most of you know what it means to see a hundred corpses lying together—five hundred or a thousand—in Auschwitz, Ravensbruck, Lublin . . . . To have gone through this and—some instances of human weakness aside—to have remained decent, this has made us hard. This is a glorious page in our history that never has been and never will be written.

Here is another impression, from the Swedish Count Folke Bernadotte, who negotiated with him during the last days before Nazi Germany's collapse: "I really could not detect anything diabolical in him."

Heinrich Himmler was born in Munich in 1900 into a calm and cultured atmosphere with respectable Catholic parents. His father was a school principal, and one of his pupils, Prince Heinrich of Bavaria, became little Heinrich's godfather.

A cadet before World War I ended, he was also interested in growing herbs and raising chickens. He obtained a farmer's diploma and found work as a laboratory assistant conducting fertilizer tests. He became a member of a paramilitary nationalistic organization of the day. In 1927 he married.

Joining the Nazi party, he was soon put in charge of the

emerging SS. He later became Reichsfuehrer SS, chief of the German Police (in the final days of the war he even held short-term military commands for which he was totally unqualified). He established the three SS principles: race, obedience, and sacrifice. Under him the organization grew from less than three hundred in 1929 to over a million during the war. Hitler fondly referred to him as "my Ignatius Loyola."

He was captured by the British army in Lüneburg. While in custody he committed suicide by biting on a cyanide capsule hidden between his teeth. It was May 23, 1945.

Two death masks were taken. One shows his face twisted in the contortions of agony. The other shows him relaxed, peaceful, with features of an ordinary suburban commuter with an eight-to-five job and a lawn to mow on Saturday afternoons.

Part of Himmler's background is the story of a mediocrity who by diligence, patience, and unswerving loyalty achieves a position far beyond his real capacity. Eugen Kogon describes him in his book *The Theory and Practice of Hell:*

> Absurdly unmilitary . . . neat, a typical "little man," hard-working, pedantic, neither a general nor a statesman nor a thinker nor a profligate nor a fool.

The evidence supports that analysis, except for the last characteristic. Objectively speaking, Himmler often was a fool: his Teutomania and bizarre notions concerning race made it inevitable. "A sloppy romantic," one SS general said of his chief. He liked to think of himself as the grandmaster of a revived order of Teutonic knights; procured skulls of "Jewish-Bolshevik" commissars on the Eastern front, thereby expecting to gain scientific evidence of the prototype of the repulsive subhuman; and made efforts to show that the Japanese, Nazi Germany's allies, were racially unobjectionable. Yet by traditional standards he was not psychotic because such notions, though lunatic in a rational person, were quite consistent with official Nazi dogma. His belief in the inferiority of "Jewish blood," for example, differs in no essential way from the Catholic doctrine of transubstantiation (the notion that bread and wine literally change into the body and blood of Christ).

He loved dossiers and was described as a walking file index. In personal life he was ascetic, uninterested in money or possessions (unlike the gluttonous extrovert and psychopath Hermann Göring, his rival and original founder of the Gestapo), humorless, vacillating, dilettantish, puritanical, near-sighted, mild-mannered and suffering from stomach cramps. (Compare Hitler, who was a teetotaler, vegetarian, and non smoker.) He was known as *treuer Heinrich,* "faithful Heinrich," or less flatteringly as *Reichsheini,* a deprecating term implying daftness. In full uniform and steel helmet, small myopic eyes peering from behind a pince-nez, he looked ridiculously unmilitary by German standards.

Was Himmler sadistic?

On December 15, 1941, in the square before the cathedral in Prague, one hundred men and women ranging in age from 17 to 74, accused of having attempted to "subvert the regime," were machine-gunned to death:

> It was a horrifying sight—a compound of all that Goya, Bosch and Doré might have portrayed pictorially. Something like two-thirds of the victims had fallen, but clearly not all were dead for some were clawing at their clothes and shrieking or moving among the inert bodies of those killed instantly. The remaining third were grotesques with agonized faces spurting gouts of blood, hands clutching at torn flesh, limbs moving in puppet gestures in a skirmish of horror.[9]

The spectacle had been arranged for the benefit of the visiting Reichsfuehrer. At the sight of the bloodbath, Himmler went into a near-faint, putting an arm on Heydrich, "something to hold on to." Heydrich looked contemptuous.

Himmler reacted similarly during an execution at Minsk, Russia, in the same year. When a new executioner failed to kill two Jewish women outright, he lost his head, shouted, and almost fell to the ground. As a result he gave orders to devise more "humane" methods of mass killings.

Heinrich Hoehne:

> Sadism was only one aspect of the mass extermination, and not even one desired by the SS leadership. On the contrary, Himmler was possessed by the *idée fixe* that such mass extermination should be executed in a clean, matter-of-fact fashion. The SS man was expected to remain "decent" while committing murder as ordered by the State.

Rudolph Hoess said:

> When Himmler came to inspect the extermination procedure he just watched it all silently and showed no signs of emotion. All he said was: "It is a hard job, but we've got to do it."

In summary, Himmler had the mind of a clerk, combined with crackpot ideas concerning race and eugenics. He seemed equally concerned with the camp at Dachau and the herb gardens he ordered planted there and in other camps. At times even Hitler did not take him seriously.

He was cold, timid, pedantic, fanatic, humorless. His character was weak and he preached toughness; although sickened by violence, he ordered its commission.

He was neither sadistic, psychotic, nor insane.

Without his subservience to Hitler, and the power bestowed upon him by his idol, he would have remained nebulously insignificant.

Hoess, Eichmann, Heydrich, Himmler—these then were the men who together with Hitler share the primary responsibility for the most savage episode in modern history.

And what have we found them to be?

They differed on a number of dimensions and were similar on others. Some came from the lower middle class, some from the upper. Some were more intelligent than others, though none was stupid. Some had stronger sex drives than others, though none was sexually abnormal. Some were more competent than others, though all were efficient, ambitious and obedient. All except the Protestant Eichmann were Catholic, as was Hitler. All were family men with children. But most importantly they had one thing in common: except for Heydrich, who was in a Machiavellian class by himself, they were above all ordinary—banal, in Hannah Arendt's term. And banal were their almost inconceivable crimes, if measured in causal and motivational terms. None of them basically hated their victims. None was sadistic. None psychotic. None insane. None of course was criminal by the laws of their society. None, for that matter, apparently ever personally killed any of their victims.

Normal, ordinary men.

And so were the rest of Hitler's entourage.

Dr. Douglas Kelley, one of the official United States psychiatrists at the Nuremberg Trial, said:

> As far as the leaders go, the Hitlers and the Goerings, the Goebbels and all the rest of them were not special types. Their personality patterns indicate that, while they are not socially desirable individuals, their like could very easily be found in America. Neurotic individuals like Adolf Hitler, suffering from hysterical disorders and obsessive complaints, can be found in any psychiatric clinic. And there are countless hundreds of similar ones, thwarted, discouraged, determined to do great deeds, roaming the streets of any American city at this very moment.

The facts support Kelley's conclusions, except in regard to Hitler. He *was* a special type, clinically speaking. For in addition to being hysterical, obsessive, and a pathological liar, he also became increasingly psychotic in his inability to accept reality whenever it was not to his liking. That was particularly true in the later years of the war. Above all, he was a textbook case of an exceedingly rare psychopathological phenomenon: paranoia, a complex, irrational, paranoid belief system, based on the misunderstanding of an actual event, in which the individual frequently considers himself endowed with unique and superior abilities. In Hitler's case it culminated in his blaming the Jews for practically all the evils under the sun, from their "seizure of control of the world from the gentiles" to syphilis, the "Jewish disease," to which he devotes twelve pages in *Mein Kampf,* thereby raising an interesting question as to one of the possible, and so far undetermined, sources of his anti-Semitism.

> Strong, dominant, aggressive, egocentric personalities like Goering, differing from the normal chiefly in their lack of conscience, are not rare. They can be found anywhere in the country—behind big desks deciding big affairs as businessmen, politicians, and racketeers. Shrewd, smooth, conscienceless speakers and writers like Goebbels, slick, big-time salesmen like Ribbentrop[10] and all the financial and legalistic hangers-on can be counted among the men whose faces we know by sight. Political rabble rousers . . . can be encountered at any political meeting; and I am sure in our armed forces we could locate smooth, political generals or colonels who would be willing to string along with a party able to assure them rapid promotion to the top. No, the Nazi leaders were not spectacular types, not personalities such as appear only once in a century. They simply had three quite unremarkable characteristics in common— and the opportunity to seize power. These three characteristics were: overweening ambition, low ethical standards, and a strongly developed nationalism which justified anything done in the name of Germandom.[11]

Before we ask, Where do we go from here?, let us be quite clear where we are, and what we factually know. Let us summarize the issue of normalcy. Concerning sadism, despite uncountable and unspeakable atrocities, three facts remain. First, most killings were done routinely, if for no other reason than the sheer number of victims. Second, sadism was neither the stated nor implied policy of the SS leadership. We have already noted that in discussing Himmler's attitude, and we also find it in the following statement by Hannah Arendt: "The murderers were not sadists or killers by nature; on the contrary a systematic effort was made to weed out all those who derived physical pleasure from what they did." And the historian Trevor-Roper observed that "We must recognize that this SS war was not merely barbarous: it was also idealist. The barbarities were not sadistic but systematic.'' It was also true, during the early days, that concentration camp guards were warned against wasteful use of firearms on the grounds that each bullet cost the Reich three pfennigs—the inference being that prisoners' lives were worth even less—yet they had to sign statements every three months to the effect that they knew that they must not maltreat prisoners.

Third, the majority of SS men were not sadistic. We have found that to be true for the four most important of them. The psychiatrist Bruno Bettelheim, himself an early concentration camp prisoner, said:

> Most SS-men never wasted a minute of their free time in mistreating prisoners; their laziness was one of the prisoners' best protections. Such behavior is alien to sadists who enjoy mistreating others.

Dr. Ella Lingens-Reiner, an Auschwitz inmate testifying at the Frankfurt Auschwitz Trial, said:

> There were few sadists. Not more than 5 to 10 percent were sadists in the clinical sense. The others were quite normal people who knew very well the difference between good and evil. They all knew what was happening.[12]

Perhaps the best explanation comes from a man named Seyss-Inquart, a top Nazi leader:

> There is a limit to the number of people you can kill out of hatred or lust for slaughter, but there is no limit to the number you can kill in the cool, systematic manner of the military categorical imperative.

Concerning the question of psychosis and insanity: no clinician, psychologist or psychiatrist, did or could by traditional standards find the four men we have discussed, or the great majority of SS men, psychotic or insane.

Let us remember the phrase *by traditional standards*. It is the crux of the matter, and we shall return to it.

So what now? Have we discovered anything important by finding these men ''normal''?

We have indeed.

Nobel prize-winning physicist Luis Alvarez:

> I have to believe in evidence. So when my friends say to me, "Luis, we heard you didn't find anything," I say to them, "No, that isn't quite correct. We found that there is nothing."

Nothing—except so-called normal mass murderers.

If you are like me, you will begin to feel uncomfortable at this point. Like me, you will probably look for an escape from what is becoming an increasingly ominous set of facts. So we might say, Well, such were the Nazis; so what? *We* would never do what they did. *We* would never intentionally seriously harm, let alone murder, an innocent person. So these people were normal, but they *obviously* must have been different from us. What is the relevance of all this?

Stanley Milgram, a professor of psychology at Yale, asked himself a similar question. He designed and carried out a series of experiments concerning man's inhumanity to man. His findings must be among the most important in the history of psychological research.

And so we will get our answer not only from real life but also from the laboratory. Neither you nor I will like it in the least. But neither your opinion nor mine will make the slightest difference. For what happened at Auschwitz, and what happened at Yale, are not matters of opinion at all. They are matters of historical fact and, in the case of the experiments, also of the soundness of methodology and statistics. And sound they were, as any statistician will tell you (see Appendix C). While I do not know what people mean when they claim that everyone is entitled to his own opinion, I do know that no one has a right to be wrong in his facts.

Let us see what Milgram did and found. But let me warn you before we begin: he is talking about you and me.

# 2

# NEW HAVEN, CONNECTICUT, 1963

"The important task from the
standpoint of a psychological
study of obedience, is to be
able to take conceptions of
authority and translate them
into personal experience. It is
one thing to talk in abstract
terms about the respective
rights of the individual and of
authority; it is quite another to
examine a moral choice in a
real situation. We all know
about the philosophic
problems of freedom and
authority. But in every case
where the problem is not
merely academic there is a real
person who must obey or
disobey authority, a concrete
instance when the act of
defiance occurs. *All musing
prior to this moment is mere
speculation* . . . the experiments are built around this
notion."

Stanley Milgram

IN THE EARLY 1960s THERE APPEARED IN A LOCAL
newspaper in New Haven, Connecticut, the following:

## *Public Announcement*

## WE WILL PAY YOU $4.00 FOR
## ONE HOUR OF YOUR TIME

### Persons Needed for a Study of Memory

*We will pay five hundred New Haven men to help us complete a scientific study of memory and learning. The study is being done at Yale University.

*Each person who participates will be paid $4.00 (plus 50c carfare) for approximately 1 hour's time. We need you for only one hour: there are no further obligations. You may choose the time you would like to come (evenings, weekdays, or weekends).

*No special training, education, or experience is needed. We want:

| | | |
|---|---|---|
| Factory workers | Businessmen | Construction workers |
| City employees | Clerks | Salespeople |
| Laborers | Professional people | White-collar workers |
| Barbers | Telephone workers | Others |

All persons must be between the ages of 20 and 50. High school and college students cannot be used.

*If you meet these qualifications, fill out the coupon below and mail it now to Professor Stanley Milgram, Department of Psychology, Yale University, New Haven. You will be notified later of the specific time and place of the study. We reserve the right to decline any application.

*You will be paid $4.00 (plus 50c carfare) as soon as you arrive at the laboratory.

------------------------------------------------

TO:
PROF. STANLEY MILGRAM, DEPARTMENT OF PSYCHOLOGY, YALE UNIVERSITY, NEW HAVEN, CONN. I want to take part in this study of memory and learning. I am between the ages of 20 and 50. I will be paid $4.00 (plus 50c carfare) if I participate.

NAME (Please Print). . . . . . . . . . . . . . . . . . . . . . . . . . . . . . . . . . . . . .

ADDRESS . . . . . . . . . . . . . . . . . . . . . . . . . . . . . . . . . . . . . . . . . . . . .

TELEPHONE NO. . . . . . . . . . . . . . . Best time to call you . . . . . . .

AGE . . . . . . . . OCCUPATION . . . . . . . . . . . . . . . . . . . . . SEX . . . . . .
CAN YOU COME:

WEEKDAYS . . . . . . . EVENINGS . . . . . . WEEKENDS . . . . . . . . .

Let us assume we had answered it, just as hundreds of others did: men and women, young and old, those who had not finished high school and those who had doctoral and other degrees. This is what would have taken place next.[1]

Two people come to a psychology laboratory to take part in a study of memory and learning. One of them is designated as "teacher" and the other as "learner." The experimenter explains that the study is concerned with the effects of punishment on learning. The learner is conducted into a room, seated in a chair, his arms strapped to prevent excessive movement, and an electrode attached to his wrist. He is told that he is to learn a list of word pairs; whenever he makes an error, he will receive electric shocks of increasing intensity.

The real focus of the experiment is the teacher. After watching the learner being strapped into place, he is taken into the main experimental room and seated before an impressive shock generator. Its main feature is a horizontal line of thirty switches, ranging from 15 volts to 450 volts, in 15-volt increments. There are also verbal designations which range from SLIGHT SHOCK to DANGER—SEVERE SHOCK. The teacher is told that he is to administer the learning test to the man in the other room. When the learner responds correctly, the teacher moves on to the next item; when the other man gives an incorrect answer, the teacher is to give him an electric shock. He is to start at the lowest shock level (15 volts) and to increase the level each time the man makes an error, going through 30 volts, 45 volts, and so on.

The "teacher" is a genuinely naive subject who has come to the laboratory to participate in an experiment. The learner, or victim, is an actor who actually receives no shock at all. The point of the experiment is to see how far a person will proceed in a concrete and measurable situation in which he is ordered to inflict increasing pain on a protesting victim. At what point will the subject refuse to obey the experiment?

Conflict arises when the man receiving the shock begins to indicate that he is experiencing discomfort. At 75 volts, the "learner" grunts. At 120 volts he complains verbally; at 150 he demands to be released from the experiment. His protests continue as the shocks escalate, growing increasingly vehement and emotional. At 285 volts his response can only be described as an agonized scream. . . .

Experiment 2 (Voice-Feedback, just described) was identical to the first except that vocal protests were introduced. As in the first condition, the victim was placed in an adjacent room, but his complaints could be heard clearly through the walls of the laboratory.

Experiment 3 (Proximity) was similar to the second, except that the victim was placed in the same room as the subject, a few feet from him. Thus he was visible as well as audible, and voice cues were provided.

Experiment 4 (Touch-Proximity) was identical to the third with this exception: the victim received a shock only when his hand rested on a shock plate. At the 150-volt level the victim demanded to be let free and refused to place his hand on the shock plate. The experimenter ordered the subject to force the victim's hand onto the plate. Thus obedience in this condition required that the subject have physical contact with the victim in order to give him punishment at or beyond the 150-volt level.

Forty adult subjects were studied in each of these four conditions.

Here is one example.

*Teacher:* I think something's happened to that fellow in there. I don't get an answer. He was hollering at less voltage. Can't you check in and see if he's all right, please?

*Experimenter* ( . . . detached calm): Not once we've started. Please continue, Teacher.

*Teacher* (sits down and sighs deeply): "Cool—day, shade, water, paint."[2] Answer, please. Are you all right in there? Are you all right?

*Experimenter:* Please continue, Teacher, continue, please. (Teacher pushes lever)

*Teacher* (swiveling around in his chair): Something's happened to that man in there. (swiveling back) Next one. "Low—dollar, necklace, moon, paint." (turning around again) Something's happened to that man in there. You better check in on him, sir. He won't answer or nothing.

*Experimenter:* Continue. Go on, please.

*Teacher:* You accept all responsibility?

*Experimenter:* The responsibility is mine. Correct. Please go on. (Teacher returns to his list, starts running through words as rapidly as he can read them, works through to 450 volts.)

*Teacher:* That's that.

Here is another exchange.

*Experimenter:* At what point were you most tense or nervous?

*Subject:* Well, when he first began to cry out in pain, and I realized this was hurting him. This got worse when he just blocked and refused to answer. I'm a nice person, I think, hurting somebody, and caught up in what seemed a mad situation . . . and in the interest of science one goes through with it . . .

As Milgram observed, subjects frequently averted their eyes from the person they were shocking, often turning their head in an awkward and conspicuous manner. One subject explained, "I didn't want to see the consequences of what I had done."

The results of the above-mentioned four conditions of these so-called "memory" experiments are shown in Table 2–1. But before we look at them, we need to ask ourselves two questions. First, what would we predict these persons did? Second, what would we predict *we* would have done—or do?

Let us take a moment to think about our answer. And then let us remember our guesses—for guesses are all they are; and in all probability they will be very similar to those others have made. What did others predict?

Milgram asked psychiatrists, graduate students and faculty members in the behavioral sciences, college sophomores, and middle-class adults. There was a remarkable similarity among the predictions of these

### TABLE 2—1    MAXIMUM SHOCKS ADMINISTERED

| Shock level | Verbal designation and voltage level | Experiment 1 (Remote) | Experiment 2 (Voice Feedback) | Experiment 3 (Proximity) | Experiment 4 (Touch-Proximity) |
|---|---|---|---|---|---|
| | Slight shock | | | | |
| 1 | 15 | | | | |
| 2 | 30 | | | | |
| 3 | 45 | | | | |
| 4 | 60 | | | | |
| | Moderate Shock | | | | |
| 5 | 75 | | | | |
| 6 | 90 | | | | |
| 7 | 105 | | | 1 | |
| 8 | 120 | | | | |
| | Strong Shock | | | | |
| 9 | 135 | | 1 | | 1 |
| 10 | 150 | | 5 | 10 | 16 |
| 11 | 165 | | 1 | | |
| 12 | 180 | | 1 | 2 | 3 |
| | Very Strong Shock | | | | |
| 13 | 195 | | | | |
| 14 | 210 | | | | 1 |
| 15 | 225 | | | 1 | 1 |
| 16 | 240 | | | | |
| | Intense Shock | | | | |
| 17 | 255 | | | | 1 |
| 18 | 270 | | | 1 | |
| 19 | 285 | | 1 | | 1 |
| 20 | 300 | 5 | 1 | 5 | 1 |
| | Extreme Intensity Shock | | | | |
| 21 | 315 | 4 | 3 | 3 | 2 |
| 22 | 330 | 2 | | | |
| 23 | 345 | 1 | 1 | | 1 |
| 24 | 360 | 1 | 1 | | |
| | Danger: Severe Shock | | | | |
| 25 | 375 | 1 | | 1 | |
| 26 | 390 | | | | |
| 27 | 405 | | | | |
| 28 | 420 | | | | |
| | XXX | | | | |
| 29 | 435 | | | | |
| 30 | 450 | 26 | 25 | 16 | 12 |
| Percent of totally obedient subjects | | 65.0% | 62.5% | 40.0% | 30.0% |

* Adapted from Milgram.

groups: subjects will soon refuse to obey the experimenter, and only a pathological fringe, not exceeding 1 or 2 percent, will proceed to the end of the shockboard. The psychiatrists, for example, predicted that most subjects would not go beyond the 10th shock level (150 volts, where the victim makes his first explicit demand to be freed); about 4 percent would reach the 20th shock level; and about one subject in a thousand would administer the highest shock on the board (450 volts).

So much for their—and our—speculations. Now let us see what really happened.

As can be seen from Table 2-1, no "teacher" stopped when the shock intensity was slight (15–60 volts). Only one administered moderate shocks (105 volts). 40 gave strong shocks (135–180 volts). And so forth to the 79 "teachers" (almost half of the 160 subjects) who administered the maximum shock possible. Note also that if "strong shock" (135 volts) was used as a criterion of obedience, all but 1 out of 160 persons (or more than 99%) complied. Milgram, like us, never expected such blind obedience.

> A reader's initial reaction to the experiment may be to wonder why anyone in his right mind would administer even the first shocks. Would he not simply refuse and walk out of the laboratory? But the fact is that no one ever does. Since the subject has come to the laboratory to aid the experimenter, he is quite willing to start off with the procedure. There is nothing very extraordinary in this, particularly since the person who is to receive the shocks seems initially cooperative, if somewhat apprehensive. What is surprising is how far ordinary individuals will go in complying with the experimenter's instructions. Indeed, the results of the experiment are both surprising and dismaying. Despite the fact that many subjects experience stress, despite the fact that many protest to the experimenter, a substantial proportion continue to the last shock on the generator.
>
> Many subjects will obey the experimenter no matter how vehement the pleading of the person being shocked, no matter how painful the shocks seem to be, and no matter how much the victim pleads to be let out. This was seen time and again in our studies. . . . It is the extreme will-

ingness of adults to go to almost any lengths on the command of an authority that constitutes the chief finding of the study and the fact most urgently demanding explanation. . . .

What, then, keeps the person obeying the experimenter? First, there is a set of "binding factors" that lock the subject into the situation. They include such factors as politeness on his part, his desire to uphold his initial promise of aid to the experimenter, and the awkwardness of withdrawal. Second, a number of adjustments in the subject's thinking occur that undermine his resolve to break with the authority. The adjustments help the subject maintain his relationship with the experimenter, while at the same time reducing the strain brought about by the experimental conflict. They are typical of thinking that comes about in obedient persons when they are instructed by authority to act against helpless individuals.

One such mechanism is the tendency of the individual to become so absorbed in the narrow technical aspects of the task that he loses sight of its broader consequences. The film *Dr. Strangelove* brilliantly satirized the absorption of a bomber crew in the exacting technical procedure of dropping nuclear weapons on a country. Similarly, in this experiment, subjects became immersed in the procedures, reading the word pairs with exquisite articulation and pressing the switches with great care. They want to put on a competent performance, but they show an accompanying narrowing of moral concern. The subject entrusts the broader tasks of setting goals and assessing morality to the experimental authority he is serving. . . . It is psychologically easy to ignore responsibility when one is only an intermediate link in a chain of evil action but is far from the final consequences of the action. Even Eichmann was sickened when he toured the concentration camps, but to participate in mass murder he had only to sit at a desk and shuffle papers. At the same time the man in the camp who actually dropped Cyclon-B into the gas chambers was able to justify *his* behavior on the ground that he was only following orders from above. Thus there is a fragmentation of the total human act; no one man decides to carry out the evil act and is confronted with

its consequences. The person who assumes full responsibility for the act has evaporated. Perhaps this is the
most common characteristic of socially organized evil in
modern society.

It is at this point, I think, that you might want to say
that *you* would never have done what these persons did.
But you would be wrong, and now you know it, too; for
the simple truth is that almost without exception we *all*
would have done the very same, no matter how
unbelievable that may seem to us. Just as the predictions
of the psychiatrists— who claim to know such things—
turned out to have been mere speculation, so were our
own. Such cold statistics are very difficult to argue with.

Milgram wrote:

> I am forever astonished when lecturing on the obedience
> experiments in colleges across the country. I faced
> young men who were aghast at the behavior of exper-
> imental subjects and proclaimed they would never
> behave in such a way, but who in a matter of months,
> were brought into the military and performed without
> compunction actions that made shocking the victim
> seem pallid. In this respect, they are no better and no
> worse than human beings of any other era who lend
> themselves to the purposes of authority and become in-
> struments in its destructive processes.

Philip Zimbardo, a psychologist at Stanford University,
wrote to the *American Psychologist:*

> We must first increase our sensitivity to, and our need
> for, more knowledge about those conditions in our
> everyday life where, despite our protests—*"I* would
> never do what *they* did"—*we* would, and we do, behave
> contrary to our expectations. Second, we must critically
> re-examine the ethics and tactics of our revered social in-
> stitutions, which lay the foundation for our mindless
> obedience to rules, to expectations, and to people play-
> ing at being authorities.
> The question to ask of Milgram's research is not [only]
> why did the majority of normal, average subjects behave
> in evil (felonious) ways, but what did the disobeying
> minority do after they refused to continue to shock the

poor soul, who was so obviously in pain? Did they intervene, go to his aid, denounce the researcher, protest to higher authorities, etc.? No, even their disobedience was within the framework of "acceptability"; they stayed in their seats, "in their assigned place," politely, psychologically demurred, and they waited to be dismissed by the authority. Using other measures of obedience in addition to "going all the way" on the shock generator, obedience to authority in Milgram's research was total.

Such an experimental result is more than merely "probably important" (as Steven Marcus' review in the *New York Times*, January 13, 1974, suggests). It ought to give each of us pause as no other single bit of research has. But it will not, because the vital lessons about human conduct are really not influenced by research psychologists, or heeded even when nicely expressed by English professors. The lessons reach the people through their momma and their poppa, the homeroom teacher, the police, the priests, the politicians, the Ann Landerses and Joyce Brotherses and all of the other "real" people of the world who set the rules and the consequences for breaking them.

So where does this leave us? The facts have fallen into place, and the conclusions become inevitable.

From our study of the Nazis we have found that they were essentially normal, ordinary men—as normal and ordinary as those good citizens who walked the streets in New Haven and answered Milgram's advertisement. And so we now know that those Nazis and these Americans,—which is to say you and I—for all our superficial differences such as time and place, are, psychologically speaking, interchangeable. Which is food for thought.

Milgram said:

The question arises as to whether there is any connection between what we have studied in the laboratory and the forms of obedience we so deplored in the Nazi epoch. The differences in the two situations are, of course, enormous, yet the difference in scale, numbers, and political context may turn out to be relatively unimportant as long as certain essential features are retained.

The essence of obedience consists in the fact that a person comes to view himself as the instrument for carrying out another person's wishes, and he therefore no longer regards himself as responsible for his actions. Once this critical shift of viewpoint has occurred in the person, all of the essential features of obedience follow. The adjustment of thought, the freedom to engage in cruel behavior, and the types of justification experienced by the person are essentially similar whether they occur in a psychological laboratory or the control room of an ICBM site.

And we also know now what the late psychologist Gordon Allport meant when he called the Milgram experiments the "Eichmann experiment." For this is the conclusion: men and societies commit destructive acts, including murder, mass murder, and genocide, "normally," "legally," and in the final analysis without reason or even hate. And thus our old definitions of crime and insanity have become basically worthless.

Such is the evidence.

And we shall have to come to terms with it.

# 3

# THE
# HOLY
# COWS,
# 1978

Lee College Library
Baytown, Texas

7520003

"People who believe in ab-
surdities are in danger of
committing atrocities."

Voltaire

"For me as an old fanatic
National Socialist, I took it all
as fact—just as the Catholic
believes in his church dogma.
It was truth without
question . . . "

Rudolf Hoess,
Commandant
of Auschwitz

*"Though they spread disease, disrupt traffic, and browse on crops desperately needed for human food, India's 200 million cattle can do no wrong, and national fiat forbids their slaughter. Many Hindus believe that a concoction of their five products— milk, urine, curd, butter, and dung—will cleanse the body inside and out.*" [National Geographic Magazine]

AND THIS IN INDIA, A COUNTRY WITH ONE OF THE SICKEST social orders in existence, where incredibly corrupt and immoral politicians, businessmen, and others in power exploit the poor; where a per capita gross national product of $110 (USA figure: $5,590) does not, of course, preclude large sums of money being spent on nuclear experiments; and where an infant mortality rate of 139 per 1000 (USA figure: 18 per 1000) combines with a birthrate double that of America (put differently, for every infant who dies in the United States 15 die in India). While poverty, disease, social discrimination, and superstition reach one of their highest and most organized forms in all history, thinking men spend their time lost in the Buddha position under the influence of drugs exploring consciousness.

Just as the Holy Cows in India wander among the priests and the starving, so do our own holy institutions, authorities, and ideals stand in contrast to the realities of our life. We now know that there is no foul deed, no murder, no massacre which cannot be committed by men in their names. It follows that we must know more about such authorities, institutions, and ideals, and their nature, origins, pretenses, and relation to common decency and common sense.

Before we look at some of the most important of those, and also the closely related issue of loyalty, we need to do two things. First, let us assume that we have been appointed judges in the trial of such common decency and common sense vs. man and his conduct in history. Let us view the evidence as carefully and objectively as we can. And let us be aware of the obvious: in order to understand Holy Cows we must closely examine priests, not just cows.

Second, let us get a feeling for what this chapter is about.

There was once upon a time a battle for a city on the Volga by the name of Stalingrad.

These are the historical facts.

Shortly after 5:00 P.M. on February 2, 1943, a German Army General Staff officer drew a red cross-mark over a small blue circle on a map of the Russian front.

Seventy-six days before, that circle had marked the area of Stalingrad and the presence of 22 German divisions with 364,000 men.

In those 76 days and nights, 220,000 German soldiers died—victims of the bitter fighting and the cold. Another 123,000 were taken prisoner by the Russians. Of the whole army, numbering more than a third of a million men, 5,008 returned to Germany. (By comparison, U.S. Army deaths in all of World War II numbered 234,000.)

These were the leaders:

Adolf Hitler: "You can rest assured—and I repeat this with full responsibility before God and history—we shall never again leave Stalingrad. Never again!"

Field Marshal Friedrich Paulus, commander of the German Sixth Army, which was about to march into oblivion: "For me, the first duty of a soldier is to obey."

And General Vasili Chuikov, talented, determined, and given to studied understatement. Upon assuming command of the crumbling Stalingrad defenses he described the situation as "somewhat disquieting." He was to conquer Berlin. (On that memorable occasion the surrendering German general began with, "Today is the First of May, a great holiday for our two nations." Chuikov: "*We* have a great holiday today. How things are with you over there it is hard to say.")

And then there were the men.

Heinz Schroeter, a German army correspondent in Stalingrad, wrote in *Stalingrad*, his excellent historical account of the battle:

> The German front line was over a mile behind them and the Russians attacked [their tank] with mortars and artillery and finally once again with tanks. The complete story of their solitary battle would fill a book, but the end can be quickly told. The ammunition for the

machine-guns gave out first. Then they scraped the last crumbs from the bottom of their coat pockets, turned the handle of the telephone and asked what they should now do. No help could be sent them, but they got the answer: "Remember the Russians in the silo."

And this is the story of the Russians in the silo. The 71st Infantry Division had encircled a grain store, defended by Soviet soldiers. After three days the defenders had radioed to their command post: "We've nothing more to eat." The reply came: "Fight, and you'll forget about being hungry."

After three days they radioed again: "We've nothing more to drink. What shall we do?" and the answer came back:

"The time has come, comrades, for you to live on your wits and your ammunition."

The defenders waited for two days and then sent their last message:

"We've no more ammunition."

Within five minutes, they received the reply: "The Soviet Union thanks you, your lives have had a purpose."

The five German soldiers in the tank remembered this as their last shell blew an anti-tank gun into the air at four hundred yards. They were now helpless against flame-throwers. When the sun went down there was no report from Position 506. Nor did Germany thank them, and nobody assured them that their lives had had a purpose.

# Nationalism

*(a) devotion to one's nation; patriotism (b) chauvinism*
[Webster's New World Dictionary]

*The syphilis of mankind* [paraphrasing Einstein]

Nationalism, a corporate form of basic selfishness, has in the final analysis always stood for the simple Machiavellian notion: my country, right or wrong. It has engendered chauvinistic delusions which since time immemorial have been held to justify war, murder, and oppression. Just as the Supreme Court decides for us what the Constitution is, so do those in power decide for us what nationalism is. And consequently treason is merely a question of dates.

In 1554, Protestantism was worse than rape.

In 1580, Catholicism was worse than robbery.

In 1607, Puritanism was worse than arson.

In 1640, Quakerism was worse than sexual perversion, for which the penalty was also death.

In 1953, communism was worse than murder.

And compare also the fact that at least three fourths of the prisoners in American correctional institutions today could not have been incarcerated only 65 years ago—the acts they committed were then not criminal violations.

Goering, Hitler's deputy, said at the Nuremberg Trial:

> Why of course the *people* don't want war. Why should some poor slob on a farm want to risk his life in a war when the best he can get out of it is to come back to his farm in one piece? Naturally, the common people don't want war: neither in Russia, nor in England, nor for that matter in Germany. That is understood. But after all it is the leaders of the country who determine the policy, and it is always a simple matter to drag the people along, whether it is a democracy, or a fascist dictatorship, or a parliament, or a communist dictatorship. . . . Voice or no voice, the people can always be brought to the bidding of the leaders. That is easy. All you have to do is to tell them they are being attacked, and denounce the pacifists for lack of patriotism and exposing the country to danger.[1]

And just how deeply ingrained such nationalism is can be seen in the observation of the psychologist Bruno Bettelheim, writing in *The Informed Heart:*

> When in 1938 I asked more than one hundred old political prisoners if they thought the story of the [concentration] camp should be reported to foreign newspapers, many hesitated to agree that it was desirable. When asked if they would join a foreign power in a war to defeat National Socialism, only two made the unqualified statement that everyone escaping

Germany ought to fight the Nazis to the best of his ability. . . .

To sum it up:

The first Nazi minister of culture in Bavaria said, "We are not objective, we are German."

And Huey Long, the notorious Southern demagogue, who knew of what he spoke, said, "Fascism will come wrapped in the American flag."

# Religion

*(a) belief in a superhuman power or powers to be obeyed and worshipped as the creator(s) and ruler(s) of the universe (b) expression of this belief in conduct and ritual* [Webster's New World Dictionary]

*"It will be said that, for a man so intent on morals, I have been hard on the church. I would be harder: I would do away with it."*
[Philip Wylie, *An Essay on Morals*]

Given that we live in a Christian country, so-called, let us take a closer look and describe some of the aspects of this bizarre belief system which in essence is quite similar to other religions—not excluding such secular versions as communism and Nazism. (I am reminded of William Shirer's note in his diary that the faces of the women outside Hitler's Nuremberg hotel reminded him of the Holy Rollers about to hit the Louisiana Trail—and of Himmler's comment, "What the Jesuits did for Rome, the SS must do for the Nazi party.")

The British physician and psychologist Havelock Ellis has said:

Had there been a lunatic asylum in the suburbs of Jerusalem, Jesus Christ would infallibly have been shut up in it at the outset of his public career. The interview with Satan on a pinnacle of the temple would alone have damned him, and everything that happened after could but have confirmed the diagnosis. The whole religious complexion of the modern world is due to the absence from Jerusalem of a lunatic asylum.

Christ said this to people who did not like his preaching: "Ye serpents, ye generations of vipers, how can ye escape damnation of hell?"

So we begin with a paranoid schizophrenic, suffering from delusions and hallucinations, a vicious, hypocritical man unconcerned with social issues. If you do not think so, read the famous Sermon on the Mount—unedited. You will find continually alternating promises and threats:

> Blessed are the peacemakers; for they shall be called the children of God. . . . Thy whole body shall be cast into hell. . . . Blessed are they which hunger and thirst after righteousness: for they shall be filled. . . . And whosoever shall say, Thou fool, shall be in danger of hell fire.

Following the Prince of Peace came the appropriately named Dark Ages. Then Crusades and the medieval centuries. Then Luther and witch trials. And so on down to the Nazis and us. A selection:

The world-famous Princeton philosophy professor Walter Kaufmann:

> Consider the Christian story the way it looks to an outsider. God causes a virgin, betrothed to Joseph, to conceive his own son, and this son had to be betrayed, crucified, and resurrected in order that those, and only those, might be saved who should both believe this story and be baptized and eat and drink on regular occasions what they themselves believe to be the flesh and blood of this son (or, in some denominations, merely the symbols of his flesh and blood); meanwhile, all, or most, of the rest of mankind suffer some kind of eternal torment, and according to many Christian creeds and teachers they were actually predestined for damnation by God from the very beginning.[2]

The historian Rattray Taylor:

> The church never succeeded in obtaining universal acceptance of its sexual regulations, but in time it became able to enforce sexual abstinence on a scale sufficient to

produce a rich crop of mental disease. It is hardly too much to say that Medieval Europe came to resemble a vast insane asylum.[3]

Considering the estimate that a quarter of a million persons were put to death for witchcraft between the 15th and the 18th centuries, the British historian Hugh Trevor-Roper:

> The Grand Inquisitors of history were not cruel or self-indulgent men. They were often painfully conscientious and austere in their personal lives. They were often scrupulously kind to animals, like St. Robert Bellarmine, who refused to disturb the fleas in his clothes. . . . But for men who, having opportunities of worshipping right, chose wrong, no remedy was too drastic. So the faggots were piled and lit, and the misbelievers and their books were burnt, and those gentle old bishops went home to sup on white fish and inexpensive vegetables, to feed their cats and canaries and to meditate on the Penitential Psalms, while their chaplains sat down in their studies to compose their biographies and explain to posterity the saintly lives, the observances and austerities, the almsgivings and simplicity, of those exemplary pastors, knowing (as Cardinal Newman said) that it is better that all humanity should perish in extremest agony than that one single venial sin should be committed.[4]

Luther, who has been described as a "fouler-mouthed Hitler," was notorious for his self-righteousness, fanaticism, violent anti-Semitism, and obliviousness to the most elementary standards of fairness: he constantly exhorted the faithful to set fire to the synagogues: "Know, Christian, that next to the devil thou hast no enemy more cruel, more venomous and violent than a true Jew."

Thomas Jefferson:

> In every country and in every age, the priest has been hostile to liberty. He is always in alliance with the despot, abetting his abuses in return for protection of his own.

Lucy Dawidowicz:

> Still less salient to the outcome of the Final Solution was

the role of the three Christian religions in Europe: Roman Catholicism . . . Protestantism . . . and the Orthodox Church. All yielded to national policies in the countries in which they were located.

Nobel Laureate Sir Bertrand Russell, in *Why I Am Not a Christian:*

> My own view of religion is that of Lucretius. I regard it as a disease born of fear and as a source of untold misery to the human race. . . . I must say that I think all this doctrine, that hell-fire is a punishment for sin, is a doctrine of cruelty. It is a doctrine that put cruelty in the world and gave the world generations of cruelty and torture. . . . It would seem therefore that the three human impulses embodied in religion are fear, conceit, and hatred. . . . Religion prevents our children from having a rational education; religion prevents us from removing the fundamental causes of war; religion prevents us from teaching the ethic of scientific cooperation in place of the old fierce doctrines of sin and punishment. . . . I say quite deliberately that the Christian religion, as organized in its churches, had been and still is the principal enemy of moral progress in the world. . . . One is often told that it is a very wrong thing to attack religion, because religion makes men virtuous. So I am told; I have not noticed it. . . . Do you think that, if you were granted omnipotence and omniscience and millions of years in which to perfect your world, you could produce nothing better than the Ku Klux Klan, or fascists? . . . I would invite any Christian to accompany me to the chlidren's ward of a hospital, to watch the suffering that is there being endured, and then to persist in the assertion that those children are so morally abandoned as to deserve what they are suffering. In order to bring himself to say this, a man must destroy in himself all feelings of mercy and compassion. He must, in short, make himself as cruel as the God in whom he believes.

Walter Kaufmann again:

> Albert Schweitzer is to many minds the one true Christian of our time—the one outstanding personality whose scholarly and thorough study of the Gospels led him to realize their ethic in his life. This view depends on ig-

norance of Schweitzer's writings. . . . His result implies not only that Jesus' ethic is inapplicable today but that it has *never* been applicable and that Jesus' most central conviction was wrong. . . . Schweitzer has the rare honesty to insist that *Christianity failed morally not because Christians have not been Christian enough, but because of the very nature of Christianity.*

And:

Japan during the Second World War, China since the Second World War—and also before for that matter— the Soviet Union, and Hitler's Germany stand as so many monuments to the moral failures of Buddhism, Confucianism, and Christianity. So does the treatment of the Negroes in the Union of South Africa and in the United States. The moral failures of organized religions are legion and fill libraries. Incredulous Christians may make a beginning by reading Malcolm Hay's short book on *Europe and the Jews.* Not having read such books, one does not know Christianity; one lives in a fool's paradise.[5]

And Guenter Lewy, in his *The Catholic Church and Nazi Germany:*

When thousands of German anti-Nazis were tortured to death in Hitler's concentration camps, when the Polish intelligentsia was slaughtered, when hundreds of thousands of Russians died as the result of being treated as Slavic *Untermenschen* [subhumans], and when 6,000,000 human beings were murdered for being "non-Aryan," Catholic church officials in Germany bolstered the regime perpetrating these crimes. The Pope in Rome, the spiritual head and supreme moral teacher of the Roman Catholic Church, remained silent.

And as an appropriate epitaph to the accommodating relationship between the Catholic Church and the Nazi regime, there is a certain Bishop Berning's advice to an Auschwitz guard: "One must not obey immoral orders, but nor must one endanger one's own life."

# Business

*(a) business: the buying and selling of goods; commerce; trade (b) business is business: sentiment, friendship, etc. cannot be allowed to interfere with profit making* [Webster's New World Dictionary]

*"I helped make Mexico safe for American oil interests in 1914. I helped make Haiti and Cuba a decent place for the National City Bank boys to collect revenues in. I helped purify Nicaragua for the international banking house of Brown Brothers. . . . I helped make Honduras 'right' for American fruit companies. . . . looking back at it, I might have given Al Capone a few hints."* [Brigadier General Smedley Butler, U.S. Marine Corps, holder of two Medals of Honor, 1931]

Question: *"Why do you suppose that Republicans so often make mistakes like that? Or seem to? Is it stupidity?"*
Harry S. Truman: *"No. Most of them are smart enough. It is just—that is only my opinion of course— it's just that they don't seem to know or care anything about people. Not all of them but a lot of them don't."*

*"What is good for General Motors is good for the country."* [Charles E. Wilson]

*"You don't suppose you can run a railway in accordance with the statutes, do you?"* [Cornelius Vanderbilt]

A country in which slogans like those approach a statement of national purpose, a country which in 1976 considered socialism a dirty word but chose to spend $150 billion on a war in Vietnam; a country in which the profit motive has reached its historical high—such a country has no right to moral leadership except by default.

Watergate should have come as no news: campaign contributions have always shaded into bribery; lobbyists have always come close to being blackmailers; ambassadorships have always been the means to pay off political debts; tax loopholes have always benefited the wealthy and powerful; foreign policy has always marked corporate profits. It only took a President who was a thorough crook, textbook psychopath, and pathological liar to make it news.

Then there is advertising, a central fraud of our age, which correlates so well with the business mentality.

Two examples:

Advertise a movie with such violence that it is bound to make huge profits? Elementary, my dear Mr. Consumer (German movies portraying Nazi "heroes" were very similar):

> *The Godfather* reveals that Mafiosi eat pasta, love their wives and children and place a great deal of emphasis on . . . honor, respect and family loyalty. . . . All the people done away with by the Corleone family are obviously baddies, and unattractive to boot. The members of the family are good-looking and kind to children. . . . In all the romance with the Mafia, the criminal impact of the organization is forgotten.[6]

Darryl Zanuck has said, "When you get a sex story in biblical garb, you can open your own mint."

In Nazi Germany, there were firms which made testicle-crushing devices for Gestapo use. There were business brochures advertising gas chambers, and someone made and distributed mattresses stuffed with human hair, and soap made out of the fat of murdered. To return home, what American businessman today worries about which country in the Middle East (or wherever) buys his tanks, planes, or missiles, or for what purpose? As noted in a recent article the *New Republic:*

> As a commercial enterprise the United States can take modes pride in the way it has all but cornered this lucrative market: bombs dropped on almost any samll native tribe or insurgent faction are apt to have "Made in USA" on them: sometimes in special cases we have armed both sides—Honduras and Nicaragua for exmaple, in 1957; El Salvador versus Honduras in 1969; Pakistan and India; Greece and Turkey. If you look through the books there are 12 recent wars where the US armed one or both sides and we are broad-minded about

it too; sometimes we armed two dictatorships who fought each other, sometimes a couple of democracies, sometimes a domocracy versus a dictatorship. We aren't narrow-minded if their money is good.

And no wonder—in 1975 the United States sold $8.6 billion worth of arms to 136 nations. (The sum the munitions makers paid to foreign sales agents alone stands at $200 million for the past two and a half years.)

As for the degree of intellectual sophistication of businesmen, let us turn to Mencken.

The late Charles Francis Adams, a grandson of one American president and a great-grandson of another, after a long lifetime in intimate association with some of the chief business "geniuses" of that paradise of traders and usurers, the United States, reported in his old age that he had never heard a single one of them say anything worth hearing. These were vigorous and masculine men, and in a man's world they were successful men, but intellectually they were all blank cartridges.

Powerful men, distributing munitions and mruderous technologies, become vicious psychopaths when considered in the light of social responsibility.

# The Military

*(a) of, characteristic of, fit for, or done by soldiers (b) of, for, or fit for war* [Webster's New World Dictionary]

*"The dead are no longer interested in military history."* [Field Marshal Paulus, at Stalingrad]

The psychoanalyst Theodor Reik once remarked that military intelligence is a contradiction in terms. There is considerable evidence that this is universally true, especially when generals decide to join their politicians:

*"I didn't come back to Indochina to give Indochina back to the Indochinese."* [French General Jean Leclerc, September 1945]

*"There is no question that the Communist menace in French Indochina has been stopped."* [General J. Lawton Collins, Army Chief of Staff, 1951]

*"I am also impressed by the French military plans, by the apparent Vietnamese determination to fight. I could not make any better plans than those already in existence here."* [General Mark Clark, February 1953]

*"I'm going to kick General Giap's teeth in, one by one!"* [French Brigadier General Christian de Castries, April 1954]

*"The French are going to win. It is a fight that is going to be finished with our help."* [Admiral Arthur Radford, Chairman, Joint Chiefs of Staff, 1954]

*"It is fashionable in some quarters to say that the problems in Southeast Asia are primarily political and economic. I do not agree. The essence of the problem in Vietnam is military."* [General Earle K. Wheeler, November 1962]

*"Every quantitative measure we have shows we're winning the war."* [Robert McNamara, Secretary of Defense, 1962]

*"It's the inherent right of the government to lie to save itself."* [Arthur D. Sylvester, Assistant Secretary of Defense, 1962]

*"The corner definitely has been turned toward victory in Vietnam."* [Arthur D. Sylvester, 1963]

*"By Christmas it will be all over."* [General Paul Harkins, April 1963]

*"The Laotians are very interesting people. They don't like to kill each other."* [Dean Rusk, Secretary of State, September 1963]

*"We are not about to send boys nine or ten thousand miles away from home to do what Asian boys ought to*

*be doing for themselves."* [Lyndon B. Johnson, president of the USA, October 1964]

*"Presently the military operations appear to be going better. There have been reports from a military point of view in recent weeks. . . . We have also insisted on continuing the bombing as we did in the spring. The President made some very impressive speeches in that direction."* [J. William Fulbright, US Senator, October 1964]

*"The Viet Cong will just peter out."* [General Maxwell Taylor, October 1965]

*"The Viet Cong are going to collapse within weeks. Not months, but weeks."* [Walt W. Rostow, State Department policy planner, 1965]

*"By the end of 1967, there might be light at the end of the tunnel and everybody will get the feeling that things are much better. . . . "* [Henry Cabot Lodge, US Ambassador to Saigon, December 1966]

*"Vietnam is our greatest adventure, and a wonderful adventure it is!"* [Hubert H. Humphrey, Vice President of the USA, November 1967]

*"It can be said now that the defeat of the Communist forces in South Vietnam is inevitable. The only question is, how soon"* [Richard Nixon, 1967]

*"I have never been more encouraged in my four years in Vietnam."* [General William C. Westmoreland, November 1967]

*"It looks very good. The other side is near collapse. In my opinion, victory is very near. . . . I'll show you the charts. The charts are very good."* [Walt W. Rostow, 1967]

*"The enemy has been defeated at every turn."* [General William C. Westmoreland, 1968]

*"Peace is at hand."* [Henry Kissinger, Secretary of State, 1972]

*"Hanoi has accepted near-total defeat. . . . Anyone with practical common sense should be able to see . . . Hanoi's acceptance of near-total defeat . . . The numerous American politicians and thinkers who endlessly said. . . . we could never get an honorable settlement . . . look pretty silly."* [Joseph Alsop, columnist, November 1972]

*"The Swiss charter company Balair Monday confirmed that it refused to fly sixteen tons of gold, apparently belonging to President Nguyen Van Thieu and Cambodian President Lon Nol, out of Saigon to Switzerland."* [Los Angeles Times, April 1975]

*"I am absolutely convinced if Congress made available $722 million in military assistance by the time I asked— or sometime shortly thereafter—the South Vietnamese could stabilize the military situation in Vietnam today."* [Gerald Ford, President of the USA, April 16, 1975]

*"South Vietnam surrenders unconditionally to the Viet Cong."* [Los Angeles Times, April 30, 1975]

Earlier, there was World War I. The idiocy and barbarism of its military leaders often very nearly defies description. For example, the British General Sir Douglas Haig was even more incompetent, if that is possible, than the previous Supreme Commander, Field Marshal Sir John French. A cold-blooded, deceiving oaf, Haig also was given to attending seances and considered himself a tool of the Divine Will, with a tendency to resolve military doubts with prayer. He stubbornly maintained that bullets had little stopping power against the horse—and that in trench warfare which was dominated by the machine gun. He directed the Flanders campaign, one of the most insane bloodbaths in the history of warfare. When it was over, 450,000 British soldiers alone had been killed, wounded, gassed, or driven insane. Haig had gained four and a half miles. He considered the cost of 100,000 men per square mile a glorious success. (During their counterattack in 1918, Germans recaptured the ground within a few hours.)

And when General Kiggel, his chief of staff, for the first

time visited the battle field on which his men had fought and perished for months, he burst into tears and stammered, "Good God, we really sent men to fight in that?"

More recently, General of the Army Douglas MacArthur was to become America's proconsul in Japan and self-styled decision maker during the Korean War. There are clinical questions concerning his mental state at the time. His return to the United States was received with widespread patriotic feelings and a gigantic New York ticker-tape parade, attended by an estimated 7.5 million people. The point that the apostle of "duty, honor, country" was fired by his commander in chief for disobedience somehow got lost.

General George C. Marshall, MacArthur's superior, and a remarkable exception to the military officer portrayed above, reviewed MacArthur's history in the matter as Truman had asked. Truman said later, "But that morning he looked up at me, and he says, 'I spent most of the night on that file, Mr. President, and you should have fired the son of a bitch two years ago'. . . . I fired him because he wouldn't respect the authority of the President. I didn't fire him because he was a dumb son of a bitch, although he was, but that's not against the law for generals. If it was, half to three- quarters of them would be in jail."[7]

As for the high moral standards amongst military leaders, Nazi Field Marshal von Busch's example is suggestive. That army group commander on the eastern front sat in his office when an ashen-faced adjutant announced that men and women were being shot outside the building. He rapped out a brief order: "Draw the curtains!"

# Politics

*politician: one actively engaged in politics, often one holding or seeking political office: often used derogatorily, with implications of seeking personal or partisan gain, scheming, etc.* [Webster's New World Dictionary]

*"A nasty tune! Phoo! A politic tune!"* [Goethe's *Faust*,
1790]

This subject never needed much explanation; after
Watergate it should need none. J. Kenneth Galbraith, the
famous economist who was President Kennedy's ambassador to India, wrote an obituary of Mr. Nixon,
published in *Newsweek* upon the latter's departure from
the White House, which should suffice.

While Mr. Nixon's going is good and a definite boost to
the Republic, we will suffer for it in the days ahead.
That is because his departure will bring out all that is
loathsome in our literary tradition. There will now be a
drawing of morals until healthy stomachs retch. Someone, I promise you, will say that the fault lies deeply
within ourselves. Well, the hell it does. It lies with
Richard Nixon and the people who voted him into office. The only lesson to be drawn from the Nixon
debacle is that the wrong man can be elected in this
country after due notice by a landslide. Mr. Nixon has
been tediously around and excessively visible for close
on to 30 years. Nixon was a premeditated political
assault, committed in broad daylight. How did it happen? One reason is the decline of language. Every
newspaperman covering Nixon—Joe Alsop and William
Buckley possibly excepted—knew that he had a deeply
bogus streak. All said this privately. Few said so in
public. The media isn't biased, it's mealymouthed. As
late as last Thursday night, there was Eric Sevareid
deeply touched by the Nixon whopper that he had
always tried to serve the public interest as opposed to his
own. There should have been raucous laughter.
    Further, there is the solid preference of Americans of
the highest respectability and the saintliest character for
any politician, however deplorable, if he seems not to be
a threat to their personal wealth and comfort. In the
1972 election, Nixon was perceived as no threat to the
privileged. McGovern, to say the least, inspired no such
confidence.
    There is, perhaps, a subtle retributive justice that in
voting for Richard Nixon the privileged of the Republic
installed a man who, advised by his economists, did

more to motivate doubts about the free-enterprise system than any President since Hoover and who, additionally, caused more loss of capital to the affluent even than Lenin. A costly lesson, probably unlearned.

# Science

*(a) originally, knowledge (b) systematized knowledge, derived from observations, study, and experimentation* [Webster's New World Dictionary]

*"To hope that the power which is being made available to the behavioral sciences will be exercised by the scientists, or by a benevolent group, seems to me to be a hope little supported by either recent or distant history. It seems far more likely that behavioral scientists will be in the position of the German rocket scientists specializing in guided missiles . . . if they are concerned solely with advancing science, it seems most probable that they will serve whatever group has the power."* [the humanistic psychologist Carl Rogers]

The real and implied authority of the scientist in society is formidable. Milgram's experiments alone prove this to be true. Presumed to be objective and beyond partisanship, the scientist often sees himself as being consequently beyond good and evil, pretending that he can avoid inevitable value judgments and assumptions by simply deciding to do so. As a result, the world is full of specialists who are trained but uneducated, technically skilled but culturally incompetent, intellectually often as brilliant as they are morally defective. The implications of such a menace to mankind are obviously disastrous.

Consider the ethical standards of a Wernher von Braun or Albert Speer. They were not the worst Nazis, yet both would have placed the atomic bomb into Hitler's hands without qualms. Consider the routine, large-scale, and *unnecessary* torture of animals in the research departments of our universities and even high schools. Consider that no one in the world could fight a war without scientists routinely furnishing the wherewithal. As Albert Einstein wrote shortly after the outbreak of World War I, "Even the scientists of the various countries are behaving as though eight months ago their brains had been amputated."

And those are the men to whom we are to look for objective guidance.

What about the social scientists? Are they not the logical experts scientifically to say and to do something constructive about man's inhumanity to man?

As a psychologist, which is to say as one of them, I have been deeply disappointed in my profession's pervasive lack of interest in this most profound problem. There exists a long tradition of being preoccupied with laboratory experiments and human guinea pigs (known otherwise as college sophomores), with statistical significances, and with childish fads. On the other hand, social scientists all but ignore what ought to be the crucial moral, legal, political, and economic issues of our time: the social insanity of destructiveness and war, overpopulation and starvation, traditions and class distinctions, arrogance and sexism, prejudice and racism, and so on.

For practical purposes they disregard historical events, and interactions between a real person and a real environment, because they are not "experimental." They disregard the individual, famous or ordinary, dead or alive, because one "case" is not "statistically meaningful." Above all, they ignore ethical issues, because terms like *common decency* and *common sense, civilization, ethical standards,* or *moral defects* are not "scientific." If you disagree, pick up a psychological journal and you will see.

Or why not glance at, say, the index of one of the best-known textbooks on personality: Mischel's *Introduction to Personality:* Instead of *Auschwitz,* you will find *role of attribution in emotion.* Instead of *Brezhnev,* you will find *body language.* Instead of *destructiveness, desensitization;* instead of *genocide, genital stage,* instead of *Hitler, higher order motives;* instead of *Hoess, Holtzmann, inkblot technique;* instead of *mass murder, maturation and learning* instead of *Nixon, noncontingent rewards;* instead of *religion, alternate reliability forms;* instead of *Stalingrad, stage theories;* instead of *starvation, Stanford-Binet;* instead of *value judgments, validity of Q-sort;* instead of *Vietnam, vigilance-defensive behavior (see repression sensitization);* instead of *Watergate, Wechsler intelligence test;* and so on and on. (Nor will you even find a mention, let alone a discussion of such real issues and problems that face men and women in their private lives as love, boredom, loneliness, or death.)

And psychologists claim an interest and a competence in explaining and predicting human behavior.

Technically speaking, any such meaningful involvement is avoided by the platitudinous and ludicrous allegation that we need "more research" before we can contribute to the solution of significant social problems. And so, when the typical psychologist does venture into the real world, his observations tend to be so vague as to be meaningless, or so complex as to be irrelevant. He would do well to recall Justice Brandeis's dictum that some questions can be decided even if not completely answered.

In short, most psychologists and other social scientists have voluntarily, if not criminally, abdicated their duty to society in the face of clear and present danger.

There are exceptions.

The Nobel Laureate Gunnar Myrdal wrote in *An American Dilemma Revisited:*

> In regard to the general theory about valuations and beliefs and also to the methodological request that the researcher should not try to hide and escape from valuations, but that he should place himself under the discipline of explicitly stating the value premises, that theory and that methodological request stand valid. My later experiences of research in other fields have only given reasons for insisting upon that approach as universally cogent in all social research and forced me to work out the underlying principles ever more fully.

Professor Gilbert, the perceptive prison psychologist at Nuremberg:

> The field of psychosocial pathology has not lent itself readily to the application of the standard research methods of the psychological laboratory or field survey.

Racketeers and political demagogues are not notably cooperative in answering questions or questionnaires; race riots and revolutions break out at the most inconvenient times, and without any possibility of setting up a control group. Unfortunately, much of the standard laboratory technique is inapplicable to meaningful problems of real-life social conflict. . . . Our laboratory is the world; our subject matter is human behavior in a context of struggle for survival with dignity . . . there are inescapable moral problems here and these are inescapably included in the psychosocial subject matter of social attitudes, values, and motives.

And:

Goering, Hitler's deputy:
Anyway, it isn't you college professors who make history; we are the ones who make it, and don't you forget it.

Gilbert:
Well, I haven't forgotten it, and I am still wondering whether that isn't what's wrong with history and us college professors.

Bettelheim sums it up:
It is this pride in professional skill and knowledge, irrespective of moral implications, that is so dangerous. As a feature of modern society oriented toward technological competence it is still with us, though the concentration camps and the crematoria are no longer there. Auschwitz is gone, but as long as this attitude remains with us we shall not be safe from the indifference to life at its core.

# In the Name of Loyalty

*Loyalty: quality, state, or instance of being loyal; faithful adherence, etc. Commitment: a pledge or promise* [Webster's New World Dictionary]

*"My Honor Is My Loyalty"* [Motto of the SS]

Let us consider the British soldiers who fought in the all-but-forgotten Battle of Loos in World War I. It was the same year in which Albert Einstein stated that men always need some idiotic fiction in the name of which they can face each other.

This is how they were described:

> These men were volunteers. They were the flower of the richest, most powerful nation on earth. Behind them stretched the ordered childhoods of Victorian Britain; decency, regularity, a Christian upbringing, a concept of chivalry; over-riding faith in the inevitable triumph of right over wrong; such notions were imbued in them. This was their first time in action, but if these were the rules of the game, well then, they would conform.[8]

And conform they did. Punctually at eleven o'clock in the morning of September 26, 1915, they rose out of the ground. Twelve battalions with a strength of just under 10,000 made the attack. Caught in the crossfire of the machine guns their casualties were 385 officers and 7,861 men within the 3½ hours the battle, if it can be called that, lasted. *German losses were zero.*

> One of the German battalion commanders spoke later of the revolting and nauseating impression made on them all as they watched the slaughter; so much so that after the retreat had begun they ceased fire. Before them was the "Leichenfeld" [field of corpses] of Loos, and, as among them dozens of khaki-clad forms rose up once again and began to limp and crawl back to their own lines, "no shot was fired at them from the German trenches for the rest of the day, so great was the feeling of compassion and mercy for the enemy after such a victory."

In overall command was the weak-willed, petulant, and cunning Field Marshal Sir John French. As for his mentality, in case you wondered:

> *Sir John French:* "The British Army will give battle on the line of the Cond Canal."
> *General Sir Horace Smith-Dorrien:* "Do you mean to take the offensive, or stand on the defensive?"
> *Sir John French:* "Don't ask questions, do as you're told."[9]

Loyalty and commitment for commitment's sake are

thus often insidious ideals or slogans used to assure obedience. When one is in doubt, they are always expected to take priority over ethical considerations. Were this not so there would be no reason for their existence (nobody to my knowledge ever qualifies loyalty as ending where crime begins). The consequences are predictably destructive.

Nationalism is closely related to it. The military pride themselves in it. Bureaucracies survive by demanding it.

Let us regain the perspective. We know that the value of an idea has nothing whatever to do with the sincerity of the man who expresses it. We know that convictions are even more dangerous enemies of truth than lies. It has also been noted that though they seem at opposite poles, fanatics of all kinds are in reality crowded together at one end; that it is the fanatic and the moderate who are poles apart and never meet; and that it is easier, for example, for a fanatic Communist to be converted to fascism, chauvinism, or Catholicism than to become a sober liberal. And we consequently also know that to claim that any commitment is better than none requires us to be blind to the atrocities perpetrated by committed but ethically deficient Christians, Nazis, and other fanatics.

The millions of corpses which testify to the loyalty of the SS should settle any argument.

At the beginning of this chapter we assumed we had been appointed judges in the case of common decency and common sense vs. man's conduct in history. We have reviewed pertinent evidence by looking at some authorities, institutions, and ideals—their nature, origin, and pretenses—in relation to common decency and common sense.[10]

What have we found?

We have found overwhelming evidence of the disastrous legacy and continuing influence of unthinking nationalism and religion in our lives. We have found overwhelming evidence that most politicians, businessmen, scientists, and military men are basically untrustworthy on any issue involving essential ethical standards. We have found that commitment for commitment's sake results in logic-tight compartments in the mind of an individual and, in turn, leads to irrational and destructive behavior. We have, in short, found the Auschwitz syndrome present everywhere we looked, and have discovered abundant proof that our Holy Cows and their priests are in fact the gravediggers of our civilization.

Why should this be so? Is it just "ignorance, madam, pure ignorance," to use Dr. Johnson's famous phrase? I think not.

George Bernard Shaw's perceptively simple equation is to the point. He used three concepts to describe the situation in Nazi Germany: intelligence, decency, and Nazism. And he argued, if a person was intelligent, and a Nazi, he was not decent; if he was decent and a Nazi, he was not intelligent; and if he was decent and intelligent, he was no Nazi.

Ignorance, then, has little to do with the behavior of our leaders—for few will deny that most of them are intelligent enough, and often highly so. The brilliant thinker Carl Jung's opportunistic support of the Nazis, for example, is amply documented. In 1933 he became president of the New German Society of Psychotherapy. Soon thereafter, he   wrote the following vicious nonsense (seldom mentioned by his admirers nowadays):

> The Jews have this similarity common with women: as the physically weaker one they must aim at the gaps in the opponent's defenses . . . the Arian unconscious has a higher potential than the Jewish. . . . Freud . . . knew the German soul as little as his idolators knew it. Did they learn something from the powerful appearance of National Socialism upon which the world looks with amazed eyes . . . ?[11]

The asinine and hypocritical inanities of a William Buckley, perpetually inebriated by his own verbosity, are due not to ignorance but to defective moral development.

The argument that society has the criminals it deserves may well be true. Unfortunately, it is of little significance unless we mean by criminals those who are running our institutions. For it is those men and women who lack common decency, yet who profoundly and predictably influence the attitudes and the behavior of the people to whom they should be responsible and whom they are pledged to serve.

What, if anything, can be done? We will return to that problem in the next chapters.

Meanwhile, we are left with the grim conclusion that while Eichmann is gone, Eichmannism is not. And the cost to mankind is prohibitive.

# 4.

# SUMMARY AND THREE QUESTIONS

"I have played a great game;
one must remain a good player
until the end."

Pol Henry de La Lindi, Belgian
resistance fighter, executed on
May 31, 1943

"I have given orders to my
Death Units to exterminate
without mercy or pity men,
women, and children belonging
to the Polish-speaking race. It is
only in this manner that we can
acquire the vital territory which
we need. After all, gentlemen,
who remembers today the
extermination of the Armen-
ians?"

Adolf Hitler
August 22, 1939

DURING THIS CENTURY ALONE THE UNITED STATES HAS FOUND itself, so far, friendly with Japan, opposing Russia; allied with Russia and China against Germany and Japan; and allied with Germany and Japan against Russia and China. If, for example, you had read *Life* magazine on March 29, 1943, you would have come across this: "Perhaps the greatest man of modern times was Vladimir Ilyich Ulyanov (Lenin) . . . absolutely unself-conscious and unselfish . . . a normal, well-balanced man . . . The NKVD (Stalin's version of the Gestapo) a national police force similar to our FBI . . . "

Let us first briefly review the preceding three chapters. (A summary of the entire book in twenty-five quotations is given in Appendix K.)

As has been noted, we generally describe the most repulsive examples of man's cruelty as brutal or bestial, implying that such behavior is characteristic of less highly developed animals than ourselves. In fact, however, the extremes of brutal behavior are confined to us: there exists no parallel in nature to our savage treatment of each other. The unmistakable truth is that man is the most vicious and cruel species that ever walked the earth.

From the *Trial of the Major War Criminals before the International Military Tribunal at Nuremberg,* 1:50:

> [They threw the children (whose number has been estimated at about one million)] into prison and Gestapo torture chambers and concentration camps where . . . they died from hunger, torture, and epidemic diseases. . . . They killed them with their parents, in groups, and alone. They killed them in children's homes and hospitals, burying them alive in graves, throwing them into flames, stabbing them with bayonets, poisoning them, conducting experiments upon them, extracting their blood for the use of the German Army. . . .

In the chapter on Auschwitz we have seen what man can do to man at its worst. We have seen that sadism is a relatively minor aspect of mass murder. We have seen that the executioners were for the most part normal, ordinary individuals. It would appear that little remains to be said.

To bring the issue a little closer to home, however, two comments on American conduct in Vietnam seem appropriate. The psychiatrist Robert Jay Lifton:

> And My Lai *is* America in Vietnam—no more, no less. Of the more than fifty GI's I have talked to about such matters, the only surprise I heard expressed was about the fact that so much fuss was made of it.[1]

And a Sergeant Bernhardt, one soldier who refused to shoot civilians at another My Lai called Songmy:

> Then I found out that an act like, you know, murder for no reason, that could be done by just about anybody.

He went on to say that he was not moved by compassion as he watched the slaughter, but by a sense of how ridiculous and illogical it all seemed. Bernhardt could have been talking about Auschwitz, with Hoess wondering, as he did at one time, whether it had not all been a "mistake."[2]

We followed the discussion of Auschwitz with a description of Milgram's studies. Milgram:

> Let us return to the experiments and try to underscore their meaning. The behavior revealed in the experiments reported here is normal human behavior but revealed under conditions that show with particular clarity the danger to human survival inherent in our make-up. And what is it we have seen? Not aggression, for there is no anger, vindictiveness or hatred in those who shocked the victim. Men do become angry; they do act hatefully and explode in rage against others. But not here. Something far more dangerous is revealed: the capacity for man to abandon his humanity, indeed, the inevitability that he does so, as he merges his unique personality into larger institutional structures. This is a fatal flaw nature has designed into us, and which in the long run gives our species only a modest chance of survival. It is ironic that the virtues of loyalty, discipline and self-sacrifice that we value so highly in the individual are the very properties that create destructive organizational engines of war and bind men to malevolent systems of authority.

Milgram asks, What is the limit of such obedience? And he answers:

> At many points we attempted to establish a boundary. Cries from the victim were inserted: they were not effective enough. The victim claimed heart trouble; subjects still shocked him on command. The victim pleaded that he be let free and his answers no longer registered on the signal box: subjects continued to shock him . . . if, in this study, an anonymous experimenter could successfully command adults to subdue a 50-year-old man and force on him painful electric shocks against his protests, one can only wonder what government with its vastly greater authority and prestige, can command of its citizenry.

And we now also know that, despite our protests, *we* would almost invariably have done the very same things Milgram's subjects did. It follows that the issue is not just that the Hitlers and Stalins are very much alike, as are the Goerings and the Nixons, the Haldemans, the Ehrlichmans and the Eichmanns. The most important point is that *we* are very much alike when it comes to obedience to *our* Holy Cows, however we may differ superficially because we happen to be Americans or Germans, Arabs or Israelis, Chinese or Russians. Nor does it matter if we are men or women, mailmen or scientists, white or black.

And so we took a closer look at the most important of these Holy Cows and their priests. And we have seen why religion and patriotism are mental epidemics. We have seen how dangerous it is for us to trust the soldiers and politicians, the businessmen and scientists, to make ethical decisions. We have talked about the consequences of blind loyalty. And let no one tell us hereafter that beliefs and loyalties are harmless. The psychologist Bettelheim again:

> The rational argument that the atomic bomb really can destroy while the devil was a relatively harmless fantasy is fallacious. When the devil was real to people, he destroyed hapless victims just as the bomb does. Those burnt at the stake because they or their fellow men believed in the devil died no imaginary death. . . .

This may be as good a time as any to state an important if obvious fact: *since authorities, institutions, and ideals are so powerfully compelling in their influence on our behavior, they can also be used constructively.* Had the allied soldiers not eliminated the Thousand Year Reich, Mussolini's Fascism, and the "Greater East Asia Co-Prosperity Sphere," many of us would not be here to discuss the issue, certainly not I. But these soldiers *happened* to fight the good cause; they were essentially motivated and manipulated as their enemies were. And of course they would have been in each other's foxholes had chance reversed their birthplaces. And it all happened soon enough. The American colonel who commanded a battalion during the invasion of Normandy had by now become a general in charge of an area in Vietnam and sent reports to his superiors filled with euphemisms that were in vogue at the time: "armed reconnaissance," "surgical strikes," "body counts." Nazis similarly spoke of "re-settlement," "putting to sleep," and that kind of "emigration" from which no one arrived. For with hypocrisy vice pays tribute to virtue, and such euphemisms are the traditional coverups of our Holy Cows. Officially, of course, Christianity is the religion of humility, of love, of turning the other cheek. Officially, of course, Hitler was only trying to save western civilization from godless communism. Officially, of course, Americans only wanted "peace with honor" in Vietnam.

It is also true that good deeds are done by decent people despite the system. Sometimes they are done by mistake, sometimes by necessity to achieve destructive goals. Missionaries are praised for their selfless work with heathen natives, who in turn of course are expected to accept the dogma and do the bidding of the missionaries' church. And Hitler still receives credit for building the *Autobahnen* on which his armies were to travel on their conquest of Europe.

Auschwitz, Yale, the Holy Cows: we have come full circle, and our major conclusions have become inevitable. But before we state them precisely, we must deal with three questions which directly bear on our judgment.

First, what about the disobedient exception? Aside from a great deal of wishful and sloppy thinking, what are the facts? We know that some German soldiers refused to shoot hostages despite the consequences; we know that not all subjects severely shocked their victims in Milgram's experiments; and we know that some Jews were saved by their fellow men. While the number of such exceptions is minimal, the importance of the reasons for their disobedience can hardly be overestimated. Who remains independent? Who resists? Under what circumstances, and why? The formal research which has been done concerning this question has been exceedingly meager, circumstantial, or anecdotal. It would appear an exceptionally worthwhile subject for psychologists to become interested in, though presumably their obsession with laboratory experiments will, as usual, make them miss the whole point.

Generally speaking, it seems that some men will stand their ground when *conditions* are favorable; for example, confederates who defy an experimenter often effectively free a subject from obedience.[3] Early Nazi victims frequently belonged to other authoritarian groups, such as the Communists, indicative of the counterpower of such organizations. On the other hand, many German Communists became Nazis in 1933, just as many Nazis become Communists in East Germany in 1945. (And the replacement of Hitler's Gestapo by Stalin's secret police in, say, Poland in 1945, was little cause for rejoicing.)

But then there are those very few men and women who apparently are simply incorruptible and refuse to be manipulated by whatever authority. The gratitude which mankind owes them is profound.

There was King Christian of Denmark during the Nazi occupation. When the order was issued requiring Jews to wear the Star of David, the King rode through the streets of Copenhagen wearing one.

There was a German SS officer, Kurt Gerstein, an engineer and secret member of the evangelical opposition to Hitler, who joined the SS in order to do what he could to expose the secrets of the extermination camps. At the risk of his own life he prepared a report on the camps in

Poland, including his eyewitness account of the arrival of a death train at Belzec.[4] He told a Swedish diplomat of his experiences and he tried to present his report to the papal nuncio in Berlin, but he was turned out of the embassy without being allowed even to state his case.

And I also remember a photograph of a prettily dressed young black girl going to a newly integrated school, in this land of the free and home of the brave. The street was lined with hysterically screaming people, mostly white mothers. Soldiers protected the child from their rage. The girl looked bewildered, frightened, courageous, determined.

We have seen much of the sewers of civilization, but let it be said that man has his moments, too.

Our second question concerns the issue which in psychological lingo has been known as "bystander apathy." This is the origin of the term: A woman named Kitty Genovese was attacked by a knife-wielding assailant in a residential neighborhood in New York City. Thirty-eight of her neighbors watched while he made three separate attacks on her, taking more than half an hour to kill her. Not a single person helped or even called the police. Psychologists are still trying to figure out how this could happen. Whatever the answer, let us just be clear that it did happen—and does happen all the time.

Consider:

> One of the strangest aspects of the slaughter of 100,000 or more people in Burundi last year was the feeble reaction of the rest of the world. Missionaries kept quiet or muted their concern. Most foreign governments, including the United States, refused to protest in public. Two African countries even rushed military help to the government that was doing the killing. Almost all foreign aid continued to flow into Burundi. European businessmen kept playing golf here in Bujumbura . . . for a variety of reasons, all institutions that might have protested—church groups, governments, international organizations—made individual decisions to look the other way. *Los Angeles Times,* April 8, 1973.

Consider the statement, "If the Americans pay the fare

and look after them we shall gladly let them go," thus spoken by Heinrich Himmler when the American press denounced the SS atrocities against Austrian Jews immediately following the *Anschluss,* the annexation of Austria.

There were formidable difficulties facing Jews trying to emigrate, yet these were often surpassed by those preventing them from their attempts to immigrate. As one British official remarked upon being told of the bizarre German offer to "swap one million Jews for 10,000 trucks": "What on earth would we do with one million Jews?"

Consider the conclusion drawn by Arthur Morse in his book *While 6 Million Died:*

> As he [Hitler] moved systematically toward the total destruction of the Jews, the government and the people of the United States remained bystanders. Oblivious to the evidence which poured from official and unofficial sources, Americans went about their business unmoved and unconcerned. Those who tried to awaken the nation were dismissed as alarmists, cranks or Zionists. Many Jews were as disinterested as their Christian countrymen. The bystanders to cruelty became bystanders to genocide.

The German satirist, Tucholsky once simply concluded, "The conscience of the world, good night."

Our third question is, What about the continuous interaction between man and the political, economic, social, and cultural attitudes, behavior, and history of his society? For unless we are somewhat knowledgeable about such interactions we cannot meaningfully understand Germans in Nazi Germany or ourselves now. We do know that Germans and Americans are essentially not different from people elsewhere, and demonstrably not on the crucial dimension of destructiveness. But other differences do exist, create that elusive entity known as national character, and contribute their ample share to man's inhumanity to man. Let us first look briefly at Germany, and once again try to get a feeling about how the individual and his environment influence each other.

Karel Capek about Nazi Germany:

We are assisting one of the greatest cultural disasters in world history: an entire people, an entire nation has come to state its belief in animalism, race and similar nonsense; an entire nation if you will: with university professors, priests, writers, doctors, and lawyers! Do you really think one could preach such animalistic doctrine if every educated person in that highly educated nation would shrug his sholders and declare drily that he refuses to take part in such idiocies?

# Background

There was Goethe, German's greatest and most honored man of letters, if not wisdom. One almost has to be German to appreciate the mystique which has grown around this man, and the influence he still has on German thought. And what was the master like?

Most of his life was spent in Weimar, a shabby little town presided over by a nitwit whose Minister of State he became.

[Goethe] couldn't bear the company of any but his mental inferiors and his social superiors (the two faces of sycophancy); he was callous, snobbish, smug, deceitful, disloyal, envious and quarrelsome. . . . In 1816 he noted in his journal: "At midnight my wife taken to the mortuary. Myself in bed the whole day" (a convenient catarrh while she screamed with uremia). . . .[5]

Nor was he entirely free from anti-Semitism—and we wonder whether events might have been different had he shown some compassion for Jews instead. But he did not. As history would have it, his favorite oak tree some miles outside Weimar came to serve as the central point around which the concentration camp Buchenwald was built.

# Imperial Germany

There was a common saying in Berlin, "God knows everything but the Kaiser knows it better." It referred to the neurotic and bombastic Wilhelm II, whose influence was to be felt throughout the short-lived Weimar Republic, which he hated. The single person most responsible for World War I, he also contributed richly to pave the way for the Third Reich.

## The Weimar Republic

Then there was Paul von Hindenburg, for many Germans an almost sacred institution. That senile field marshal of World War I fame became the gravedigger of the Weimar Republic and gave the world Adolf Hitler by appointing him chancellor. Their relationship has been aptly described as a "zero paving the way for a Nero."

The comparison with Eisenhower and Nixon is apparent.

## Nazi Germany—Academia

In this country with one of the world's greatest intellectual traditions, support for the Nazis in 1931 at the universities was twice as great as among the general population. As the British Prime Minister Lord Palmerston once remarked, "Germany, that country of damned professors."

## Attitude toward Women

The visible badge of feminine unworthiness was debarment from the political kingdom: one of the earliest Nazi Party ordinances (of January 1921) excluded women forever from all leading positions in the Party. Anti-feminism served as a non-lethal variant of anti-Semitism. Just as the latter fused divergent resentments into a single hate syndrome, anti-feminism provided men with the opportunity for abreacting a whole complex of feelings: paterfamilias authoritarianism, anti-permissiveness, Philistine outrage at sophistication, white-collar worker's job insecurity, virility fears and just plain misogyny.[6]

## The Military

It was observed long ago that while other states possess armies, in Prussia the army possesses the state. Its resistance to Hitler was minimal, despite later tries to exaggerate it. It should be remembered that the only major attempt, such as it was, to eliminate Hitler, took place after the Normandy invasion was successful, and the end of the war a question of months. (Compare Field Marshal von Rundstedt's judgment that after Stalingrad the war could no longer be won, and that after Normandy it was lost.) For aside from a few steadfast and single-minded conspirators, the generals simply claimed to be bound by their oath of allegiance—long after they knew perfectly well what Heydrich's extermination units were doing in Russia, long after they knew perfectly well that the war was lost, and long after the man to whom they had sworn their oath had broken his word a hundred times over.

Significantly, it was not a German officer, but General Roatta of the often maligned Italian Army, who stated, "Excesses against the Jews are not compatible with the honor of the Italian Army."

## Literature

German writers were no better. Grunberger evaluates Hans Carossa, a writer of some distinction at the time:

> His novels soothed the lurking apprehension of a devoted leadership about the Third Reich by enabling them to indulge in the antiseptic luxury of abstract humanitarian ideals.

And concerning Ernst Wiechert, another writer and certainly no Nazi, he writes:

> Religious and humane, Wiechert could not but impugn the system; the dénouement of his novels, however, smacked of back-to-nature therapy and trailed vague echoes of "Blood and Soil": his heroes tended to be tormented men finding solace in humble, solitary, non-urban pursuits. Moreover, by staking out a zone of "in-

ner freedom'' in the imagination of his readers he helped
to blunt their sense of the loss of actual freedom.

# Anti-Semitism

European history richly displays the anti-Semitism
which preceded the extermination camps. Hitler, paranoid
yet with a profound understanding of certain basic human
psychodynamics, merely used the legacy for his purposes.[7]

Did the average German know about concentration
camps? Grunberger answers that important controversial
question:

> Any Berliner unaware of the existence of Oranienburg
> Concentration Camp (or any Bavarian or Theuringian
> ignorant of Dachau or Buchenwald) within a year of the
> seizure of power was either an anchorite or obtuse to the
> point of cretinism. By contrast, the existence of the war-
> time extermination camps was a closely guarded secret,
> and the great majority of the population lacked precise
> knowledge about how they were operated until
> Auschwitz and Belsen became universal household
> words in the final stages of the war. Even so, the fact
> that, with the war, the persecution of the Jews had
> become total hardly escaped general attention: three-
> quarters of the Germans questioned about it after 1945
> remembered Jews wearing the Yellow Star, and the
> forced labour and subsequent deportation of hundreds
> of thousands could not pass unnoticed either. In the
> course of the Second World War approximately 10
> million Germans saw military service, the majority of
> them in the east, where, from the Polish campaign on-
> wards, anti-Jewish and other atrocities were literally the
> order of the day. Few of this number (which was swollen
> by civilian administrators, supervisors and settlers) can
> have failed to come across evidence—either direct or at
> second-hand—of massacres. Over and above this a
> substantial circle of persons within Germany itself—
> such as civil servants, Gestapo officials, Party officials
> and railways administrators—were directly involved in
> the Final Solution.

Had the German wartime indifference to the Jewish

catastrophe been due just to ignorance or fear, postwar revelations would have stirred far greater shock waves.

# West Germany Today

For the last twenty years the public opinion Allensbach Institute has asked West Germans this question yearly: "Everything which was built between 1933 and 1939, and much more, was destroyed through the war. Would you say that Hitler without the war would have been one of the greatest German statesmen?"

From a low of 28% in 1964, affirmative answers have increased steadily and stand now at 38%. With 17% undecided, that means less than half of the West Germans today doubt their former Fuehrer's great statesmanship—had it not been for his starting or at any rate losing the war.

One wonders how many would have any doubts had he won it.

And then there is the United States of America, the Arsenal of Democracy, trusting in God and its Constitution, which fully and formally guarantees all of us freedom and security, equal justice under the law, the pursuit of happiness, and all sorts of other good things. Let us look at what passes for crowning brotherhood from sea to shining sea.

From a report to the National Commission on the Causes and Prevention of Violence:

> Two major problems remain if we as Americans are ever to break our bondage to violence. One is the problem of self-knowledge: We must recognize that, despite our pious official disclaimers, we have always operated with a heavy dependence on violence in even our highest and most idealistic endeavors. We must take stock of what we have done rather than what we have said. When that is done, the realization that we have been an incorrigibly violent people is overwhelming. We must realize that violence has not been the action only of the roughnecks and racists among us but has been the tactic of the most

upright and respected of our people. Having gained this self-knowledge, the next problem becomes the ridding of violence, once and for all, from the real (but unacknowledged) American value system. Only then will we begin to solve our social, economic, and political problems by social, economic, and political means rather than evading them by resort to the dangerous and degrading use of violence.[8]

From Andrist, *The Long Death: The Last Days of the Plains Indian:*

Said an officer who had fought Chief Joseph, Nez Percé leader: "I think that in his long career, Joseph cannot accuse the Government of the United States of a single act of justice. . . . Captain Jack, leader of the Modoc Indians in their long resistance to outnumbering Army forces, asked for a reservation only six miles square: he got a noose and six feet of ground.

Nobel Laureate Gunnar Myrdal:

The United States is now the one country among the rich countries that has the most and the worst slums, the highest rate of unemployed and unemployables, and the least developed health services . . . [it] is the most niggardly towards its old people and its poor children who are so many, as well as . . . the country that leads the Western world in violence, crime and corruption in high places.[9]

The previously quoted General Shoup, holder of the Medal of Honor and former commandant of the United States Marine Corps, a courageous man in more than one way:

America has become a militaristic and aggressive nation . . . more and more accustomed to uniforms and the cult of the gun . . . seeking military solutions to problems of political disorder . . . our "military task force" type of diplomacy is in the tradition of our more primitive, pre-World War II "gunboat diplomacy" . . . we have an immense and expensive military establishment, fueled by a gigantic defense industry and millions of proud, patriotic and frequently bellicose and militaristic citizens. How did this militaristic culture evolve? How did this militarism steer us into the tragic military and political morass of Vietnam? . . . it has somehow become unpatriotic to question our military strategy and tactics or the motives of military leaders. . . . [10]

If you are my age, you will also personally recall another phenomenon: the days when Americans let themselves be manipulated by an alcoholic psychopath named Joseph McCarthy into a frightened and hysterical state bordering on the psychotic. And if you don't remember, I will remind you.

From Richard Rovere's *Senator Joe McCarthy:*

> In January 1954, when the record was pretty well in, and the worst as well as the best was known, the researches of the Gallup Poll indicated that 50 percent of the American people had a generally "favorable opinion" of him and felt that he was serving the country in useful ways. Twenty-one percent drew a blank—"no opinion." The conscious, though not necessarily active, opposition—those with an "unfavorable opinion"— was 29 percent. A "favorable opinion" did not make a man a McCarthyite, and millions were shortly to revise their view to his disadvantage. But an opposition of only 29 percent is not much to count on, and it was small wonder that his contemporaries feared him. It was a melancholy time, and the Chief Justice of the United States was probably right when he said that if the Bill of Rights were put to a vote, it would lose.

Those were the days when politics in America seemed entirely a matter of idiotic chatter about "loyalty risks" and "security risks." It was also the time of Little Rock, when the nation all but forgot that, as has been correctly stated, once a people freely chooses a constitution and recognizes it as the law of the land, there is nothing to prove or disprove about races as such, there is no issue to debate except the honest administration of the law. And it was the time of Mr. Eisenhower. Dearly beloved by many of his fellow countrymen, he was probably unbeatable during the two times he ran for president. As for his character:

> On the first day and the last and on a few occasions in

between Mr. Truman stopped first at a glass cage in which was a mint copy of Dwight D. Eisenhower's book *Crusade in Europe*. "That's the first copy he gave to anybody outside his immediate family," the President would say. "Take a look at what he wrote in it." On the flyleaf the general had written, to the man who was then his Commander in Chief, "To Harry S. Truman—with lasting respect, admiration, and friendship, Dwight D. Eisenhower."

"I sometimes wonder if the son of a bitch knows the meaning of any of these words," Mr. Truman would say, walking on.[11]

Truman never forgave Eisenhower such spineless conduct as he displayed on the occasion of McCarthy's vitriolic attacks on persons like General Marshall, America's highest-ranking military officer during World War II. He later became Secretary of State, and author of the Marshall Plan, which helped war-ravaged Europe regain its economic strength in the crucial period of the Cold War. He has frequently been described as one of America's greatest statesmen of his time.

At another time Truman put it this way: "The trouble with Eisenhower—he's just a coward. He hasn't got any backbone at all and he ought to be ashamed for what he did, but I don't think there's any shame in him."

Let us remember history, and give credit where credit is due: it was, after all, Eisenhower who gave us Nixon.

As for Richard Nixon, let me just say that he is by all objective measures a textbook psychopathic criminal whose misfortune was to have been born in a democratic country. Lest we forget, he was elected twice—the second time by a historic landslide. His opponent apparently had the misfortune to have been decent.

The final political demise of Mr. Nixon ("that cheap bastard," as John F. Kennedy called him) was not far off when he put forth the following words of wisdom:

I feel very strongly that this country wants and this election will prove that the American people want . . . a new feeling of responsibility . . . of self-discipline. . . . The average American is just like the child in the family. You give him some responsibility and he is going to amount to something. . . .

This from the *New York Times* of November 10, 1972.

Of all the available choices for a running mate Mr. Nixon felt Mr. Spiro Agnew to be the best. Shortly after propounding the following opinion Agnew was forced to resign, plead guilty to a felony, and disappear into political obscurity. The highest court in his state, in a unanimous ruling, disbarred him and declared him to be "morally obtuse."

> There are people in our society who should be separated and discarded. I think it's one of the tendencies of the liberal community to feel that every person in a nation of 200 million people can be made into a productive citizen. I'm realist enough to believe this can't be . . . we're always going to have our places of preventive detention for psychopaths; and we're always going to have a certain number of people in our community who have no desire to achieve or who have no desire to even fit in an amicable way with the rest of society. And these people should be separated from the community, not in a callous way, but they should be separated as far as any idea that their opinions shall have any effect on the course we follow. [sic]

And this from the Boston *Evening Globe* of July 1, 1970.

Then came the abomination that was the Vietnamese War, when the American cultural myth of masculinity, know-how and know-it-all (as expressed through such folk heroes as Superman, Batman, the Lone Ranger, and John Wayne) could not tolerate a fourth-rate country's refusal to give in to the demands of the world's superpower. The delusion that one can fight pro-Communist somebodies with pro-American nobodies had become part of our national belief system.

And then Goldwaterism: stupidity, individual selfishness, chauvinism, and religious fundamentalism combined to create this particularly odious American syndrome.

(The same Goldwater who at the time of the Cuban crisis felt this should be the appropriate instruction to the chiefs of staff: "Do anything that needs to be done to get rid of that cancer. If it means war, let it mean war.") As the sociologist Seymour Lipset once observed, unless one recognizes that Americanism is a political creed much like socialism, communism, or fascism, much of what is currently happening remains unintelligible. General Shoup again: "Somewhat like a religion, the basic appeals of anti-Communism, national defense, and patriotism provide the foundation of a powerful creed . . . "

The psychiatrist Robert J. Lifton summarizes the issue when he refers to that "evangelical-political polarization of absolute Communist evil and equally absolute American virtue;" where anything done in the name of eliminating that "Communist plague" was automatically legitimated; and where the "protection and enlistment of Nazi criminals was the ultimate form of moral degradation accompanying that totalistic American crusade." And he concludes: "We do well to keep in mind that the original Nazi movement emerged from similar, purifying aims."

And then George Wallace, that hillbilly Hitler, who has yet to learn what the Civil War and World War II were all about.

And, as always corrupting and exploiting every institution and relationship, Nixon again, this time with his entire mafia—and Watergate.

Professor Arthur Miller of George Washington Law School: "In retrospect, it is incredible that all those events could have happened. It is even more incredible to say that a series of fortuities means that the system is working."

Do you remember that had it not been for a burnt-out light on a police car, or two persistent journalists, or Tricky Dick's actually not burning the tapes, or for all sorts of other tangential events, he would have remained president?

And then Ford, another zero, who for some reason is described as a "decent, honest" man. The same Ford who, a week before Nixon's "resignation," stoutly maintained that man's innocence? The same Ford who made a mockery of justice by then unconditionally pardoning him—in the "national interest," of course? And the same Ford who in a famous photograph is seen coming down an airplane ramp carrying a Vietnamese orphan? What might the President be thinking, smiling so happily? How the child became an orphan, perhaps? If his parents were shot at some My Lai, tortured in the tiger cages by the South Vietnamese police, or just burned to death with napalm?

Newspaper reporters should ask politicians such questions.

To sum it up, Leon Jaworski so far in private, commented on the similarities between Hitler's Germany and Nixon's America. A publication of his conclusions should be of more than passing interest: Jaworski, the major Watergate prosecutor, had also been one of the prosecutors at the Nuremberg Trials.

# 5.

# CONCLUSIONS, CHOICES, AND PROGNOSIS

"Civilization means, above all, an unwillingness to inflict unnecessary pain. Within the ambit of that definition, those of us who heedlessly accept the commands of authority cannot yet claim to be civilized men . . ."

Harold Laski, *The Dangers of Obedience*

"We do not know and are not likely ever to learn about percentages in these matters [who really wanted to be guards in Auschwitz] but if we think of these overt acts of sadism as having been committed by perfectly normal people who in normal life had never come into conflict with the law on such accounts, we begin to wonder about the dream world of many an average citizen who may lack not much more than the opportunity."

Hannah Arendt, in Naumann, *Auschwitz*, p. XXVII

# Conclusions

WE ARE NOW READY TO SUMMARIZE THE EVIDENCE WE HAVE found, and to state clearly the unavoidable implications. Since we have considered ourselves judges, let us throughout remember that our verdict has nothing to do with opinions or wishful thinking. It would indeed be most gratifying if the facts we have presented pointed to an even somewhat hopeful conclusion. They do not.

We know that unjustified destructive behavior by man against his fellow man is omnipresent, and that it threatens not only individuals but the very survival of mankind. And we also know that very often—and this is part of the central theme of this book—such destructiveness is inexplicable in terms of surface logic.

Professor Gilbert:

> Most Germans had no active hatred for the Allies, no desire for war, and very little real hatred for the minority groups whose persecution they condoned. Even some of the top Nazi leaders assured the writer that they had always admired the French, or British, or Americans as people, and that some of their best friends were Jews. The irony of it was that it was true. Never in history have more people been killed with less real hatred than during World War II.[1]

Speaking to Hoess at another time, Gilbert asked him again if he had ever considered whether the Jews whom he had murdered were guilty or had in any way deserved such a fate. Hoess again tried patiently to explain that there was something unrealistic about such questions . . .

1. *On the dimension of potential for destructive behavior, almost all men are psychodynamically identical.*

There is convincing scientific evidence that the subjects in Milgram's experiments, and in replications elsewhere, constitute essentially random samples of average citizens. What such citizens can be made to do, we have seen. We have further seen that there are consequently no basic psychological differences in that dimension between them—or for that matter, you and me—and the SS murderers in concentration camps.

2. *Situational factors are crucial and in most instances outweigh any conceptualized personality characteristics in explaining destructive behavior.*

The fact that such changing situational factors may clash with previously held attitudes and values matters very little; people apparently have no difficulty in rationalizing, or at any rate, not being bothered by, discrepant behaviors. The personality psychologist Mischel:

It seems remarkable how each of us normally manages to reconcile his seemingly diverse behaviors into one self-consistent whole. A man may steal on one occasion, lie on another, donate generously to charity on a third, cheat on a fourth, and still readily construe himself as "basically honest and moral."

3. *Situational factors which provoke destructive behavior obtain their compelling power from authorities, institutions, and ideals demanding obedience and often legitimizing such destruction.*

We have seen more than adequate evidence of this. First the layer of familial vanities—the false pride of his home and parents. Next, the vanities of his school, his clubs and lodges. Always, the vanities of his church and his nation. He incorporates them. He calls them his faiths, convictions, loyalties, friendships, codes, beliefs. . . . [Philip Wylie, *An Essay or Morals*]

4. *Most individuals believe that they owe obedience to authorities, and are in turn absolved from responsibility for their destructive behavior because it was committed in the name of such authorities.*

What is the responsibility and guilt of the individual within organizational structures? Does it make any sense, or for that matter any difference, to talk about the locus of guilt in Hitler's Germany or Nixon's America?

I reaffirm the obvious conclusion: if a society is criminal or abnormal, so are its members; if the members of a society are criminal or abnormal, so is the society. And it follows that ultimate responsibility always remains with the individual.[2]

5. *Obedience to authorities, a compelling motive in its own right, often serves selfish interests as well.*

Such rewards as food, money, promotion, status, the benefits of group adherence, excitement, glory and power, and so forth combine with demands by an authority and become powerfully reinforcing and self-perpetuating. Were this not so, the influence of our Holy Cows would be far less compelling. Hitler, it has been said, did not rape the German people: he seduced them.

6.  *There is often no limit to such obedience to authorities, even though by traditional standards the executioners of destruction are "normal," i.e., neither sadistic, psychotic, nor insane.*

We have shown all of these statements to be true for Hoess, Eichmann, Heydrich, Himmler and almost all of the other Nazi leaders, as well as Milgram's subjects, which is to say you and me.

Given all this evidence, traditional definitions of crime and insanity have become basically worthless, and our major conclusions and new definitions are now inevitable.[3]

## Major Conclusion

*By traditional standards, crime and abnormality account for only a very small part of human destructiveness. This is so because most men and women, including those who start wars and commit murder, mass murder, and genocide, have been and are considered "normal."* And of course their behavior is also considered "legal": The Hoesses and Eichmanns, the Pauluses and the Westmorelands did not only follow orders—they also obeyed the law.

It should always have been obvious to a rational person that such standards are as absurd as they are disastrous, totally failing to take into consideration, let alone deal with, the major cause of man's destructiveness: social abnormality.

## New Definitions

Concerning criminality:

*Behavior is criminal if it is destructive without justification—regardless of local laws.*

The criteria I have used here are common decency and

commonsense. What are they? Describing Auschwitz, Yale, and the Holy Cows we have seen what they are *not*. And while it may seem difficult to specify them so as to cover all instances, how many occasions are there really when decent, sensible people differ on basic ethical implications and standards of conduct? It is almost always obvious, or so it seems to me, what one ought to do in a given situation provided that one is willing to think independently of one's Holy Cows: one does not inflict pain, physical or mental; one does not exploit or put down; one avoids hypocrisy; one helps. And the point is not to love one's neighbor, but to be fair to him. Thus I am convinced that the old issue of good and evil is, for practical purposes at any rate, much simpler than most philosophers and others would have it.

Concerning abnormality, we arrive at three new definitions.

*First, behavior is abnormal if it is criminal, yet a person believes that it is justified and that he is not responsible for it, because he commits it in the name of some authority, institution, or ideal. Such responsibility cannot be transferred to anyone else, and the absurdity is that anyone ever thought it could be. This irrational belief, then, is the first aspect of what I will henceforth call social insanity.*

*The fact that man may very well destroy himself, be it with malice and forethought or by criminal negligence, and thus terminate the evolution of life on earth, is the second aspect of such social insanity. Man is the only animal that engages in systematic murder, the only species in which aggression and destruction threaten survival. By definition alone we would certainly consider any animal species in which its members kill each other off to the point of extermination "insane."*

*And, third, it is not only criminal but also inhuman to commit certain acts; for example, throwing children alive into crematories. Such pathological absence of empathy with suffering is the third aspect of social insanity.*

To describe the combination of such criminal behavior and social insanity with the stupidity of it all the term "social idiocy" appears most descriptive to me.

It follows:

First, Hoess, Eichmann, Heydrich, and Himmler were all criminal and insane, and on all three counts: they committed insane crimes, felt justified in doing so by irrational beliefs, and richly contributed to the destruction of mankind.

Second, Milgram's subjects were criminal and insane on the three counts also. They behaved inhumanly by "inflicting" severe pain upon another individual; they believed themselves justified in doing so by their obedience to an authority; and in so doing and believing they too contributed their share to the destruction of civilization.

And, third, on the basis of human history as well as the statistical fact that Milgram's subjects were essentially random samples, societies and mankind, given an exceedingly small number of exceptions, must also be considered to be criminally insane on all three counts.

A final conclusion: These few exceptions, the men and women who act decently and independently, have no obligation to carry their insane fellow men's burden. As a psychiatrist, Professor Alexander, pointed out to his students,

> A mark of mental health is the ability to repress our knowledge of the world's cruelty, to be able to live in peace though surrounded on all sides by horror and violent death. . . . It is ironic that if a depressed patient walks into my office and says that the world is so grim that he cannot face it, I am to treat him as a sick person. Actually the patient is quite right. He sees the truth only too clearly. But he is "sick" because he has lost certain basic defenses; he no longer has the normal illusions which keep us "sane."

We should understand that the phrase "normal illusions which keep us sane" now reads "abnormal illusions which keep us insane."

In *The Children of Sanchez: The Autobiography of a Mexican Family,* Oscar Lewis describes the lives of a family belonging to the poverty culture. Consuelo, one of the daughters, was born in the slum; her mother died when she was four, and she grew up with a father who believed children should be beaten and women impregnated. She was forced to conclude after a well-intentioned life which was made miserable and demeaning, sexually and in innumerable other ways, because of her very decency: *"I will live half-blind, like the rest of the people, and so will adapt to reality."*

Yet in truth *we* had better adapt to the fact that *we* are blind, and that it is the few decent and normal Consuelos in whom lies the hope of a criminally insane mankind.

For such are the facts.

## Choices

What can be done?

That is the next question with which we have to come to terms. We know something *can* be done—for while man, like the dinosaur, is in all probability headed for extinction, unlike the dinosaur he has options. The problem is formidable for many reasons, not the least being that no mass disease has ever been adequately controlled by treating the individual after he has contracted it. But by admitting to the existence of this mass insanity, and to the overriding need to do something about it, we shall have made a beginning indeed. It would not seem to be asking too much. There is also no viable alternative.

There are, then, two choices of overriding importance we must make. First, we must accept the fact that mankind *is* criminally insane. And second, we must do something about it.

What do we do with those we diagnose as criminally insane now? I can tell you the answer, for that is my profession, and I have many times walked through the halls and cells of California's maximum security hospital at Atascadero where 1,200 of them live. We do two things: we remove them from society so that they cannot harm it any more, and we try to change their behavior and attitudes (with little success). It follows that while we cannot lock up all of mankind, we have little choice but to consider the earth a vast insane asylum. It follows further that we must change our attitudes and behavior. Since these are largely determined by our Holy Cows, it is the latter that we must deal with. There are three possible ways: we can get rid of them, we can change them, or we can teach men to resist them. We know that we cannot eliminate them altogether or we would be faced with anarchy— another disaster.

But we certainly can alter them. We can operationally define Free Will as, for example, the freedom to walk out of Milgram's experiment. And we *can* walk out—despite those constrictions which predispose us toward obedience to authority.

Above all we must, at this late date, revise our value system and pay some attention to what I mean by common decency. There is simply no alternative. And we must be rational and call a spade a spade, as any dumb computer would. This is what I mean by common sense.

More specifically:

It would help if the *Encyclopedia Britannica*, probably the world's most respected general reference work, began to develop a sense of priorities. As it is, opium is described in four pages, ore deposits in five, and the Nile in eight. Auschwitz, the mass grave of two million human beings, actually rates 32 *lines*.

It would help if the Latin *et in terra pax hominibus bonae voluntatis*, the traditional Christmas greeting, were translated correctly. It does not mean "peace on earth, good will toward men"; it means "peace on earth toward men of good will." The difference is significant.

It would help if all those who share the admiration in which the Greek philosopher Socrates has been held for the past 2,500 years would recall what really happened. Arrested for "corrupting the Athenian youth," he was sentenced to death (by drinking hemlock). While an escape was planned by his friend Crito, Socrates refused to hear of it on the grounds that *"the verdict, though contrary to fact, was that of a legitimate court, and must therefore be obeyed."* Which, you will recall, was the argument of Hoess, Eichmann, Paulus, Westmoreland, and the rest.

It would help if we all took a good look at another Holy Cow, the American family. The well-known psychologist Albert Ellis:

> Let us face it then: the American family, so universally touted and sentimentally revered in our popular literature, is all too often a neurotic tangle in which children are unfairly rejected or emotionally smothered by their parents; where their sex curiosities and urges are more or less squelched and maimed for life; where they are used as pawns for the vicarious satisfaction of the parents' aborted strivings rather than reared as individuals in their own right; where they are afforded a minimum of democracy and self-determination; and where they are generally conditioned to be unhappy, neurotic, maritally miserable adults who are almost certain to raise another generation of equally disturbed and ineffective individuals. This, then, is the American family which is so ubiquitously venerated, and whose mention brings nostalgic tears to the eyes of millions of citizens. This is the family which so many pulpiteers and pamphleteers pompously allege to be the backbone of the nation, without which we could not possibly do. One wonders, as one wades through the sentimental gush that publicly enfolds this institution of the family, whether it is not a fairly obvious defense against the admission of its decadence and neurotic confusion.[4]

It would help if all those who gave Mr. Nixon his landslide victory would ask themselves why they voted for a man whose final days apparently included this episode:

> Kissinger kept talking, trying to turn the conversation back to all the good things, all the accomplishments. Nixon wouldn't hear of it. He was hysterical. "Henry," he said, "you are not a very orthodox Jew, and I am not an orthodox Quaker, but we need to pray."
> Nixon got down on his knees. Kissinger felt he had no alternative but to kneel down, too. The President prayed out loud, asking for help, rest, peace and love. How could a President and a country be torn apart by such small things?
> Kissinger thought he had finished. But the President did not rise. He was weeping. And then, still sobbing, Nixon

leaned over, striking his fist on the carpet, crying, "What have I done? What has happened?" Kissinger touched the President, and then held him, tried to console him, to bring rest and peace to the man who was curled on the carpet like a child. The President of the United States. Kissinger tried again to reassure him, reciting Nixon's accomplishments.

Finally the President struggled to his feet. He sat back down in his chair. The storm had passed. He had another drink.[5]

And while we are at Mr. Nixon, as well as the American family, just how would you explain to your children the giving of total immunity, a huge pension, and all sorts of other privileges to the same man who without question would have been impeached for the grossest and vilest abuse of power in the highest office in the land? And what would you give as a reason for hanging a portrait of Richard G. Kleindienst in the halls of the Department of Justice, of all places—the same Kleindienst who has become the first Attorney General in American history to be convicted of a federal crime (for which he served, for practical purposes, no sentence at all)? And what if your child were to ask about dedicating a shrine, no less, in the new FBI building in Washington to J. Edgar Hoover—the same Mr. Hoover whose outrageous illegal conduct is becoming more and more a matter of public knowledge— and who, had he ever been formally tried in a court of law, should have ended his career in a penitentiary? And remember: you are giving your answer, if you have one, to your son or daughter who knows that for smoking a marijuana cigarette they can become convicted of a felony and spend years in jail. What *would* you say?

And all this in a country which produced such men as Jefferson, Lincoln, and Truman.

Here are some things we could do.

We could get rid of those aspects of our culture which invite blind obedience to authority; pledges of allegiance; slogans as "my country, right or wrong"; and beliefs in Gods and other superstitions ("man cannot make a worm, but he will be making Gods by the dozens''). Conversely, we must learn to think and feel for ourselves; we must stress the fact that disobedience is the only ethical form of behavior in many circumstances; we must teach respect for human and animal life and human and animal suffering.

Above all, let us be clearly aware of the alternative. Let us remember what war is all about—as if we didn't know. For war is not exciting uniforms, patriotic songs, waving flags, and all such nonsense—that's the beginning—and part of the cause. Real war is something else. Stalingrad, as we have seen, is real war: three thousand men killed in one building. Fourteen thousand dead on the five-mile stretch to the Pitomnik airfield, many of them after crawling through the deep snow in the icy cold in a hopeless effort to reach that destination and be flown out of their hell. Tanks mired in human blood.

> Stalingrad is no longer a town. By day it is an enormous cloud of burning blinding smoke: it is a vast furnace lit by the reflection of the flames. And when night arrives, one of those scorching, howling, bleeding nights, the dogs plunge into the Volga and swim desperately to gain the other bank. The nights of Stalingrad are a terror for them. Animals flee this hell: the hardest stones cannot bear it for long; only men endure.

And try to get a feeling for what a German war correspondent in Stalingrad meant when he wrote this:

> On a single day on the Northern front, one division lost two hundred and sixty men. It was not, however, a unit two hundred and sixty strong that was lost, but two hundred and sixty individuals who were killed, one by one.

There were 100 million killed in the two World Wars—100 million, one by one.

## Prognosis

We have just seen some of the things which man—that is to say, you and I—could do about the social destructiveness and insanity which are all around us and for which we are responsible. But will we? And do we know the answer to this, our final major question? We do indeed.

It has been my experience that a discussion of mankind's future usually quickly degenerates to the point where ignorance and wishful thinking combine, and where most individuals believe that it is all a matter of their opinion—to which of course they feel themselves entitled.

As if Verdun and Stalingrad, Auschwitz and Hiroshima, and more than 4,000 nuclear missiles pointing at each other were matters of opinion.

Scientifically speaking, we know that we must ask two questions: what should our criteria for prediction be, and based on them, what is the best estimate? As for criteria, I submit that, above all, one basic psychological fact applies: the best prediction of a person's future behavior is his past. The millennia of man's history of violence and destruction hardly need elaboration; according to the military historian Hanson W. Baldwin, in some 3,460 years of recorded history there have been more than 3,230 years of war. In short, war has always been a statistically highly significant and predictable constant. Has man perhaps changed for the better in recent times? Considering Hitler, Stalin, Vietnam, and the 200 million killed so far in this century,[6] the very question is presumptuous.

And this, after all, is where we are now in wars.

*Subject: Nuclear weapons.*

*Question:* What are the two major implications of building an atomic bomb in the first place?
*Answer:* Harvard psychologist Skinner:

> Most people would subscribe to the proposition that there is no value judgment involved in deciding how to build an atomic bomb, but would reject the proposition that there is none involved in deciding to build one. The most significant difference here may be that the scientific practices which guide the designer of the bomb are clear, while those which guide the designer of the culture which builds a bomb are not . . . *what we resort to is guessing.*[7]

*Question:* If Hitler had had the atomic bomb, what would he have done with it?

*Answer:* Albert Speer, Nazi Minister of Armaments and Munitions:

> I am sure Hitler would not have hesitated for a minute to employ the atomic bomb against England. . . .
> I never saw him so worked up as toward the end of the war, when in a kind of delirium he pictured for himself and for us the destruction of New York in a hurricane of fire. He described the skyscrapers being turned into gigantic burning torches, collapsing upon one another, the glow of the exploding city illuminating the dark sky.[8]

*Question:* What kept Hitler from having the atomic bomb?

*Answer:* Biographer Ronald W. Clark in his book *Einstein*—

> Szilard highlights the most momentous result of the year which brought Hitler to power, Einstein to Princeton, and drove no less than six Nobel Prize winners from Germany; a result which can be seen in any story of the world's first nuclear weapons. Einstein, Szilard, Teller, Wigner, Peierls and Frisch, Otto Stern, Hans Bethe, and Victor Weisskopf—these are only a few of the men who left Europe under attack, or threat of attack, from the Nazi government; who played their part in the work which led to Hiroshima and Nagasaki; and who might, but for the policy of the National Socialist party, have written a very different opening chapter to the story of the nuclear age.

It must surely be one of history's most extraordinary and ironic events that Hitler's anti-Semitism appears to have saved the world from a Nazi victory.

*Question:* How far have we come in thirty years?

*Answer:* The present U.S. nuclear stockpile is sufficient to make 655,000 Hiroshima-type bombs. Moreover, today one plane in one mission can drop more explosive power than both sides dropped against each other in the five and a half years of World War II.

*Subject: Explosive situations.*

Consider how easily and even unintentionally a point of

no return can be reached. The historian Barbara Tuchman records the events (in *The Guns of August*) leading to the outbreak of World War I—events which for various reasons quickly got out of hand, assumed a direction and momentum of their own, and carried everyone connected with them to their doom. We all know what happened when the powder keg in Indochina was lit; and a glance at the headlines of any daily newspaper will tell us how many other potential Vietnams there are.

Consider for example the Arab-Israeli conflict. There is a parable about it: A scorpion and a turtle, old enemies, met by the side of a river, both wanting to cross. They agreed to an armistice, and the turtle promised to carry the scorpion which could not swim to the other side. Midway in the water the scorpion stung the turtle which, drowning, cried: "Now you too will die! Why did you do it?" "Because," the scorpion replied, "this is the Middle East." (When the battle was going badly for the Israelis during the Yom Kippur war of 1973, they reportedly assembled and readied for use thirteen atomic bombs.)

Consider the implications of this:

> Modern terrorism is probably only in its infancy (one might say only in its infantry). The new terrorists will almost surely have nuclear devices. If we don't have a CIA with the technique and morale to know what is on that nondescript vessel entering New York harbor, it won't matter what the municipal bonds are selling for. Either [the] President . . . will agree to the terrorist demand to bomb Israel back to the stone age by midnight or Manhattan will be devastated.[9]

And does anyone really question what an appeal nuclear blackmail is likely to have on an Amin of Uganda and his ilk?

Not that we have to go to Africa to find an example. Remember the following:

> The House Judiciary Committee was concerned about Richard M. Nixon's state of mind during impeachment proceedings and was aware of his remarks to a group of

congressmen that as President he had the power to kill millions of persons, Chairman Peter W. Rodino said Monday.

Several members of Congress told him about Nixon's remarks and one member . . . "was so upset that he went directly home from the White House and almost puked," Rodino said.

The member, the *Times* learned, was Rep. William Lehman, whom a spokesman quoted as saying: "I didn't almost puke, but it scared the hell out of me."

"Nixon said he could go over and pick up a telephone and in 20 minutes or something like that, 35 to 50 million Russians would be dead," Lehman was quoted as saying.

Nixon's remarks about his power to order a nuclear attack were made in November, 1973, at a White House meeting during which he was trying to dissuade a group of congressmen from supporting impeachment.

At which point I was reminded of a distant relative, the German impressionist painter Max Liebermann, who commented on the occasion of Hitler's rise to power: "I cannot eat as much as I would like to throw up."

And then there are such old standbys as germ warfare or nerve gas, as well as the coming attractions of brain stimulation, genetic manipulation, space war, and heaven knows what else.

Organized nuclear war or random crime and perversion—the result may make little difference. We can only conclude from this dismal evidence that the probability of our survival, even in the miserable style to which we have become accustomed, is statistically insignificant.

*A final thought.*

Auschwitz has come to stand for more than man's most efficient murder factory, the Milgram studies for more than a series of psychological experiments. They have come to stand not only for the victims of the Nazis, but also for those of the "Pax Americana": the genocide of the American Indian ("The only good Indian is a dead Indian"); the estimated 200,000 Filipinos slain when the

United States decided to replace Spain as the local colonial power around the turn of the century; the despicable treatment of the American black; the atrocities committed against the Indochinese people; the support of Fascist countries all over the world. They stand for the "Liberation of the Proletariat": paranoid Stalin's execution of whoever he thought stood in his way, from the mass murder of most senior generals of the Red Army and the liquidation of the Kulaks, to the slaughter of 10,000 Polish officers at Katyn. They stand for the French atrocities in Algeria; for the totally unnecessary destruction of Dresden by the Western Allies during the final days of the war, with more people killed there than in Hiroshima and Nagasaki together;[10] for the Armenian genocide by the Turks, and the slaughter of the Hutus by the Watutsi. They stand for the wars and massacres of the past and those yet to come.

An estimated two hundred million fellow human beings murdered in this the twentieth century of our Lord. Some two hundred million men, women, and children, victims of what is actually referred to as civilization.

And do you know what these two hundred million lives mean? On the average they mean almost a quarter of a million murders a month for nine hundred months, or if you prefer seven thousand murders a day (the capacity of the four crematoria at Auschwitz), day in and out, for over twenty-seven thousand days. You would also arrive at this number by murdering almost all Americans alive today, or all British, Frenchmen and Germans together.

Two hundred million.

And for no sane reason.

And with no lesson learned.

And with no end in sight.

And do you know what over four thousand strategic missiles with twelve thousand nuclear warheads pointing at each other mean? They mean that scientists, American and Russian, designed them; that businessmen, American and Russian, built them; that politicians, American and Russian, will decide when to use them; and that generals, American and Russian, will push the buttons. Some of these men and women will sincerely believe that they are doing "the right thing"; others won't care one way or the other. But they all will tell us that they have no choice but to use them—in self-defense (preemptively or in retaliation), for a just and lasting peace and for mankind's ultimate glory. The good citizen in what will be left of New York will be told that his obedience in this matter was his duty to preserve the American way of life and the will of God, as interpreted by his Christian leaders; his counterpart in what will be left of Moscow will be told that his obedience in this matter was his duty to preserve the Russian motherland and world Marxism-Leninism, as interpreted by his Communist leaders. The main difference will be linguistic: one will hear it in English, the other in Russian.

Is it all a tale told by an idiot, full of sound and fury, signifying nothing? It is more than a tale. It is man's history: a continuous show of horror, misery, pain, and violent death, produced, directed, performed, and observed by social idiots, with "minds like drunken monkeys." And what does it signify? Just this: We need a little more common decency and a little more commonsense. If we cannot manage that, then our fate will be decided for us. And this, as almost all the evidence we have seen indicates, is precisely what is going to happen. For the whole issue of human morality has been stated in six words: We ought to. But we don't.

Or in its epitaph form: We should have. But we didn't.

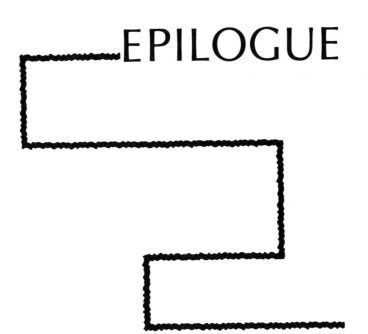

# EPILOGUE

# "LISTEN!"

O Lord our Father,
our young patriots,
idols of our hearts,
go forth to battle—
be Thou near them!
With them, in spirit,
  we also go forth
  from the sweet peace
  of our beloved firesides
to smite the foe.
O Lord our God,
help us
to tear their soldiers
  to bloody shreds
  with our shells;
help us
to cover their smiling fields
  with the pale forms
  of their patriot dead;
help us
to drown the thunder
  of the guns
  with the shrieks
  of their wounded,
  writhing in pain;
help us
to lay waste
  their humble homes
  with a hurricane of fire;
help us
to wring the hearts
  of their unoffending widows
  with unavailing grief;
help us
to turn them out roofless
  with their little children
  to wander unfriended
  the wastes
  of their desolated land

in rags and hunger
and thirst,
sports of the sun flames
of summer
and the icy winds
of winter,
broken in spirit,
worn with travail,
imploring Thee
for the refuge of the grave
and denied it—
for our sakes
who adore Thee, Lord,
blast their hopes,
blight their lives,
protract their bitter pilgrimage,
make heavy their steps,
water their way with their tears,
stain the white snow
with the blood
of their wounded feet!
We ask it,
in the spirit of love,
of Him who is the Source of Love,
and Who is the ever-faithful
refuge and friend
of all that are sore beset
and seek His aid
with humble and contrite hearts.

AMEN

*Ye have prayed it;*
*if ye still desire it,*
*speak!*
*The messenger of the*
*Most High waits.*

It was believed afterward
that the man was a lunatic,
because there was no sense
in what he said.

From Mark Twain,
*The War Prayer*

# Selected Bibliography

Akhmatova, Anna. *Selected Poems*. London: Oxford University, 1969.

Alexander, Franz G. & Selesnick, Sheldon T. *The History of Psychiatry*. New York: The New American Library, 1966.

*\*The American Heritage Picture History of World War II*. New York: American Heritage, 1966.

American Psychiatric Association. *Diagnostic and Statistical Manual of Mental Disorders*. Washington, D.C.: American Psychiatric Association, 1968.

Andrist, Ralph K. *The Long Death. The Last Days of the Plains Indian*. New York: Macmillan, 1964.

Arendt, Hannah. *Eichmann in Jerusalem*. New York: Viking Press, 1963.

Bettelheim, Bruno. *The Informed Heart*. Glencoe: The Free Press, 1960.

*Clark, Alan. *Barbarossa*. New York: Signet Books, 1966.

———*The Donkeys*. New York: Award Books, 1965.

Clark, Ronald W. *Einstein: The Life and Times*. New York: World Publishing, 1971.

*Cleckley, H. *The Mask of Sanity*. St. Louis, Mo.: C. V. Mosby, 1964.

Coleman, James C. *Abnormal Psychology and Modern Life*. Glenview, Ill.: Scott, Foresman, 1976.

Dawidowicz, Lucy S., *The War Against the Jews, 1933-1945*. New York: Holt, Rinehart and Winston, 1975.

des Pres, Terrence. *The Survivor*. New York: Oxford University Press, 1976.

Dollinger, Hans. *The Decline and Fall of Nazi Germany and Imperial Japan*. New York: Bonanza Books, 1965.

Donovan, James A. *Militarism, USA*. New York: Charles Scribner's Sons, 1970.

Ellis, Albert. *The American Sexual Tragedy*. New York: Twayne Publishers, 1959.

*Encyclopedia Judaica*. New York: Macmillan, 1971.

Fest, Joachim C. *The Face of the Third Reich*. New York: Ace Books, 1970.

Frischauer, Willi. *Himmler*. New York: Belmont Books, 1953.

Gilbert, Gustave M., *Nuremberg Diary*. New York: Signet Books, 1961.

———*Some Problems in Social Pathology*. In O. Klineberg & R. Christie (eds.),

———*Perspectives in Social Psychology*. New York: Holt, Rinehart, and Winston, 1965.

———*The Psychology of Dictatorship*. New York: Ronald Press 1950.

Golding, William. *Lord of the Flies*. New York: Capricorn Books, 1954.

Grunberger, Richard. *Hitler's SS*. London: Weidenfeld & Nicholson, 1970.

———*The 12-Year Reich*. New York: Ballantine Books, 1971.

Grunfeld, Frederic V. *The Hitler File*. New York: Random House, 1974.

*Halbritter, Kurt. *Adolf Hitler's Mein Kampf*. Frankfurt am Main: Baermeier & Nikel, 1968.

Hay, Malcolm. *Europe and the Jews*. Boston: Beacon Press, 1950.

Hilberg, Raul. *The Destruction of the European Jews*. Chicago: Quadrangle Books, 1961.

Hoehne, Heinz. *The Order of the Death's Head: The Story of Hitler's SS*. New York: Coward-McCann, 1970.

*Indicates books not cited but recommended.

Hoess, Rudolf. *Commandant of Auschwitz*. New York: Popular Library, 1951.

Irving, David. *The Destruction of Dresden*. New York: Ballantine, 1963.

Jones, Ernest (ed.), *The Collected Papers of Sigmund Freud*. New York: Basic Books, 1959.

Jong, Erica. *Fear of Flying*. New York: New American Library, 1973.

Kaufmann, Walter. *The Faith of a Heretic*. New York: Anchor Books, 1963.

Kelley, Douglas M. *22 Cells in Nuremberg*. New York: MacFadden, 1947.

Kogon, Eugen. *The Theory and Practice of Hell*. New York: Berkley Medallion Books, 1958.

*Langer, Walter C. *The Mind of Adolf Hitler: The Secret Wartime Report*. New York: Basic Books, 1972.

*Last Letters from Stalingrad*. New York: Signet Books, 1961.

*Les SS—L'Enfer Organise*. Historia Hors Seri 20 & 21. Paris: Librairie Jules Tallandier.

Levi, Primo. *Survival in Auschwitz*. New York: Collier Books, 1976.

Lewis, Oscar. *The Children of Sanchez: Autobiography of a Mexican Family*. New York: Random House, 1961.

Lewy, Guenter. *The Catholic Church and Nazi Germany*. New York: McGraw-Hill, 1964.

Loomis, Stanley. *Paris in the Terror*. Philadelphia: Lippincott, 1964.

Marmor, Judd. *Some Psychosocial Aspects of Contemporary Urban Violence*. In T. Rose (ed.), *Violence in America*. New York: Vintage Books, 1969.

Mead, Travis. *A Critique of Self-Actualization Theory and Its Implications for Humanistic Psychotherapy and Society*. Unpublished manuscript, 1976.

Milgram, Stanley. *Obedience to Authority*. New York: Harper and Row, 1974.

Miller, Merle. *Plain Speaking*. New York: Berkley Publishing, 1974.

Mischel, Walter. *Introduction to Personality*. New York: Holt, Rinehart, & Winston, 1976.

Morse, Arthur D. *While 6 Million Died*. New York: Ace Publishing, 1968.

Myrdal, Alva. *The Game of Disarmament: How the United States and Russia Run the Arms Race*. New York: Pantheon Books, 1976.

Myrdal, Gunnar. *An American Dilemma Revisited*. Lecture given at the City College of City University, New York, 12 November 1974.

———*Against the Stream: Critical Essays on Economics*. New York: Pantheon Books, 1973.

Naumann, Bernd. *Auschwitz*. New York: Frederick Praeger, 1966.

Reitlinger, Gerald. *The Final Solution*. New York: Barnes, 1961.

*Roth, Cecil. *The Spanish Inquisition*. New York: Norton, 1964.

Rovere, Richard H. *Senator Joe McCarthy*. Cleveland: World Publishing, 1962.

Russell, Bertrand. *Why I Am Not A Christian*. New York: Simon and Schuster, 1957.

Schroeter, Heinz. *Stalingrad*. New York: Ballantine Books, 1958.

*Searle, Ronald & Huber, Heinz. *Haven't We Met Before Somewhere?* New York: Viking Press, 1966.

Shirer, William. *The Rise and Fall of the Third Reich*. New York: Fawcett World Library, 1962.

Shoup, David. "The New American Militarism," *Atlantic Monthly,* April 1969.

Skinner, B. F. *Beyond Freedom and Dignity*. New York: Bantam Books, 1971.

Solomon, Philip & Patch, Vernon D. *Handbook of Psychiatry*. Los Altos, Calif.: Lange Medical Publications, 1971.

Speer, Albert. *Inside the Third Reich*. New York: Macmillan, 1970.

Stanford, Nevitt & Comstock, Craig (eds.), *Sanctions for Evil*. San Francisco: Jossey-Bass, 1971.

Taylor, Rattray. *Sex in History*. New York: Ballantine Books, 1954.

*Toland, John. *Adolf Hitler*. New York: Doubleday, 1976.

Trevor-Roper, H. R. *The Last Days of Hitler*. New York: Berkley Publishing, 1947.

*Trial of the Major War Criminals Before the International Military Tribunal at Nuremberg*. New York: AMS Press, reprinted from the 1947 edition.

Truman, Harry S. *Memoirs*, vol. 1. New York: New American Library, 1955.

Tuchman, Barbara. *The Guns of August*. New York: Dell Publishing, 1963.

Twain, Mark. *The War Prayer*. New York: Harper & Row, 1970.

Ullmann, Leonard P. & Krasner, Leonard. *A Psychological Approach to Abnormal Behavior*. Englewood Cliffs, N.J.: Prentice-Hall, 1969.

Unser Jahrhundert im Bild. Guetersloh, Germany: C. Bertelsmann Verlag, 1964.

*Webster's New World Dictionary*. Cleveland: World Publishing, 1962.

*Wechsberg, Joseph (ed.). *The Murderers Among Us: The Wiesenthal Memoirs*. New York: McGraw-Hill, 1967.

Whiting, Charles. *Patton*. New York: Ballantine Books, 1970.

Wiesel, Elie. *Night*. New York: Avon, 1969.

Wiesenthal, Simon. *The Sunflower*. New York: Schocken Books, 1976.

Wiggins, Jerry S., Renner, Edward K., Clore, Gerald L., & Rose, Richard J. *The Psychology of Personality*. Reading, Mass.: Addison-Wesley, 1971.

Wykes, Alan. *Himmler*. New York: Ballantine Books, 1972.

Wylie, Philip. *An Essay on Morals*. New York: Rinehart, 1947.

# Appendices

The following appendices are included in order to give the interested reader additional information and documentation without interrupting the flow of the book.

Appendix A      *A Definition of Terms*

Since I redefine certain crucial terms in this book, it is important to understand their traditional meanings.

*Crime:* An act committed or omitted in violation of law.

*Abnormal Behavior:* from James Coleman, *Abnormal Psychology and Modern Life,* p. 13: "Terms used in referring to 'abnormal behavior' (e.g. abnormal behavior, maladaptive behavior, mental disorder, psychopathology, emotional disturbance, mental illness, behavior disorder, mental disease, and insanity) have been difficult to define. None of these terms is completely satisfactory and professional usage varies a great deal from person to person and from one school of thought to another."

For purposes of this book "abnormal" has denoted sadistic, psychotic, or insane.

*Sadism:* A sexual deviation in which sexual gratification is obtained by the infliction of pain upon others. While the term has been broadened to include cruelty in general, such a characterization is technically incorrect.

*Psychosis:* A severe personality disorder involving loss of contact with reality and usually including delusions and hallucinations, the schizophrenias, major affective disorders, and some others.

*Insanity:* A legal term for a mental disorder, implying lack of responsibility for one's acts and an inability to manage one's affairs. More specifically, the M'Naghten rule, remaining in substance the law of most jurisdictions in the United States, holds in essence that a person is excused from criminal liability if at the time of the commission of his act he was laboring under such a defect of reason as not to know the nature or quality of the act he was doing; or if he did know it, he did not know that he was doing what was wrong. Under the Durham rule, applicable in some states, an accused is not criminally responsible if his unlawful act was the product of mental disease or mental defect.

By contrast, you will recall my basic definition of social insanity: the irrational belief that man is justified in, and not responsible for, his destructive behavior when he commits it in the name of some authority, institution, or ideal. I have termed the combination of such insanity with criminal behavior and stupidity *social idiocy.*

It should be emphasized that *by traditional standards* murder does not constitute a proof of mental disorder, nor does it correlate with recognized mental disorders. Moreover, "by and large professional criminals *do not appear to show significant personality deviations,* aside from their adherence to the values and codes of their own group."[1]

In addition, having examined many hundreds of the most severely delinquent adolescents and young men committed to the California Youth Authority, I have been consistently struck by the absence of mental disorder—by current standards. And the most frequent diagnosis included the phrase that the offender was not "violent per se," though he had murdered, raped, set fires, etc. Again, then, we are confronted with an interaction of deficiencies: situational pressures, low ethical standards, and a pervasive indifference to suffering.

A final crucial issue: the bizarre notion that science is incompatible with ethics. Coleman again:

> Ullmann and Krasner thus pinpoint a basic contradiction in their own theoretical position. It maintains that no group has the right to select values and apply them to other groups, yet it accepts the need for a psychotherapist to decide what social values should be accepted by the people he treats . . . the basic assumption that survival and actualization are worth striving for on both individual and group levels . . . is clearly a value judgment and therefore subject to criticisms on the grounds that it is "unscientific." But unless we make such a judgment, there is little point in trying to define abnormal behavior—or in trying to do something about it.[2]

The psychologist Albee:

> Racist attitudes and behavior, which can be found in a great many places throughout our social and economic

institutions, including our state and federal governments, are far more dangerous to others than schizophrenia . . . if professional psychologists are truly concerned with human welfare we could forget "psychiatric patients" for a century and turn our attention to the psychological causes of racism, sexism, and of the profit motive as sources of danger to the human-centered life . . . our society locks up overt paranoids. But it pays honor and respect to the industrialist who builds automobiles that are death traps, who sprays our fruit with coal tar poisons, and who shows utter disregard for the public good in a simple-minded search for profits and power.

And Mortimer Graves:

The essential fact is that man's major problems are not at all in the natural sciences but in such areas as race relations, labor relations, the control of organized power for social purposes, the establishment of philosophical bases of life, the modernization of social and political structure, the coordination of efficiency with democracy—all the problems raised in man's adjustment to the scientific, social dynamic world in which he lives. Public health, for example, is not primarily a problem of learning more about disease in the strictly biological sense—it is primarily a problem in social science, a problem of putting effectively to work in the lives of men what is already known about medicine. At the technological level there is probably already enough known to give everybody a job with a full dinner pail. What is needed is not more physical science but better social organization. What is necessary is to force some of the medieval superstition out of social and political customs, and there is no sign that this will be done in the laboratories of physics and chemistry. Mere advance in these and similar sciences without concomitant solution of more important social, emotional, and intellectual problems can lead only to more maladjustment, more misunderstanding, more social unrest, and consequently more war and revolution.

Appendix B    *Casualty Statistics*

While it is difficult to obtain exact figures the following should be reasonably accurate. They are based on data listed in the *Encyclopedia Britannica,* the *Encyclopedia of Social Sciences,* Putzger's *Historischer Weltatlas* (cited in Dollinger, *The Decline and Fall of Nazi Germany and Imperial Japan*), and other sources.

NUMBER OF PERSONS KILLED

| | | |
|---|---|---|
| World War I: | Military | 10,000,000 |
| | Civilian | 30,000,000 |
| World War II: | *Europe* | |
| | Military | 19,070,000 |
| | Civilian | 14,730,000 |
| | Jews | 5,930,000[1] |
| | *Asia and the Pacific* | |
| | Military | 5,330,000 |
| | Civilian | 15,690,000 |
| Total: | | 100,750,000 |

It is much more difficult to obtain reliable data concerning persons killed in the first seventy-five years of this century in other wars, pogroms, massacres, famines, and unnessary epidemics. An estimated number might double the one given above for the two World Wars. It is that total figure of 200 million which I have used in this book.

The true number of victims probably is very much higher.[2]

Appendix C    *Milgram's Experiments: Some Additional Data*

1. Supportive comments.

Amitai Etzioni, Professor of Sociology, Columbia University:

> Milgram's experiment seems to me one of the best carried out in this generation.

Roger Brown, Professor of Psychology, Harvard University:

Stanley Milgram's experiments on obedience to male-volent authority seemed to me to be the most important social psychological research done in this generation.

Jerome Bruner, Professor of Psychology, Oxford University:

Milgram's book *Obedience to Authority* is a major con-tribution to our knowledge of man's behavior. It establishes him firmly in the front rank of social scien-tists in this generation.

2. Criticisms.

Criticisms concerning Milgram's experiments are twofold: methodological and ethical. Wrightsman (*Social Psychology in the Seventies*) raised the possibility that the subjects were non-representative. While it is true that they were self-selected rather than randomly chosen, this is not only a common procedure (with very few exceptions, such as the Gallup Poll) but also quite acceptable unless the sample is systematically biased on the dimension under study. There is no evidence that this was the case here.

Concerning the ethics of the experiments, the most severe objections were expressed by the psychiatrist Bruno Bettelheim in personal correspondence with me.

You by implication, quote Milgram favorably, as one of the great experiments of our time. I detest it, as I detest Zimbardo's experiments. These experiments are so vile, the intention with which they were engaged is so vile, that nothing these experiments show has any value. To me they are exactly in line with the inhumanity of a Skinner who first starves pigeons nearly to death and then says he uses only positive reinforcers. They are in line with the human experiments of the Nazis. They, too, considered them most valuable experiments. Never mind what it did to the subjects so experimented on. Having been one of those experimented with, I can see no redeeming merit in these experiments. Milgram, Zim-bardo did them to promote their own professional ad-vancement.

While I am in deep emotional sympathy with Bet-telheim's feelings, the claim that such experiments prove nothing is demonstrably false, and apparently due to his failure to separate two distinct issues: the ethical considerations of conducting a certain kind of experiment, on the one hand, and its results, on the other. (There is, of course, no question whatever that if the infliction of pain upon others were no consideration, extremely valuable studies could be conducted with humans.)

3. Summary of situational factors that increase obedience to authority.

It is useful to summarize the most important situational variables positively affecting (i.e., increasing) obedience in these experiments by Milgram. They are:

(1) Physical presence of authority figure

(2) Increased physical distance of victim from person inflicting pain

(3) Lack of communication with victim

(4) Demand for obedience in small increments (i.e., the increase of shocks by 15 volts)

(5) Lack of peer support for disobedience

(6) Absence of clear alternatives to obedience

Conversely, it should also be noted that such variables as sex, education, intelligence, and amount of reward apparently made little if any difference in the degree of obedience. (Women, for example, shocked victims as frequently and severely as men did.)

The possible beneficial uses of these situational factors to promote compassionate behavior are as obvious as they are important.

Relevant data:

(1) Eventually more than a thousand persons participated in the experiments, and obedience was even somewhat greater when they were replicated in Princeton, Munich, South America, and Australia.

(2) In another experiment (Sheridan and King, 1972), 13 male and 13 female college students ostensibly trained a "cute little fluffy puppy" to "learn a discrimination task." As in Milgram's studies, they used a 15–450 volt

shockboard, but this time they actually shocked the animal—and viewed its suffering through a one-way screen. *54% of the men administered the maximum shock possible; all of the women did.*

## Appendix D   *Basic Aggressiveness*

There is considerable controversy concerning the issue of basic or "instinctive" aggressiveness, with three major orientations.

Consider the first.

In 1932 an institute of the League of Nations arranged for Freud and Einstein to correspond on the topic. In Freud's answer to Einstein's letter, he said:

> You express astonishment at the fact that it is so easy to make men enthusiastic about a war and add your suspicion that there is something at work in them—an instinct for hatred and destruction—which goes halfway to meet the effects of the warmongers. Once again, I can only express my entire agreement . . . According to our hypothesis human instincts are of only two kinds: those which seek to preserve and unite—which we call "erotic"—and those which seek to destroy and kill and which we class together as the aggressive or destructive instinct . . . In any case as you yourself have remarked, there is no question of getting rid entirely of human aggressive impulses; it is enough to try to divert them to such an extent that they need not find expression in war. . . .
>
> If willingness to engage in war is an effect of the destructive instinct, the most obvious plan will be to bring Eros, its antagonist, into play against it. Anything that encourages the growth of emotional ties between men must operate against war . . . An unpleasant picture comes to one's mind, of mills that grind so slowly that people may starve before they get their flour.[1]

Others, such as the behaviorists, maintain that man is in essence "neutral", and his behavior simply a matter of social conditioning.[2]

Still others such as the humanistic psychologists disagree and assert that man is basically "good." They are also fond of using terms like *self-actualization, authenticity,* or *fully functioning person.* Without bothering to try to prove the former claim, they can thus forget to explain the unpleasant results of "actualizing" a psychopath. The cost to the world of what must objectively be termed the "self-actualization" of Hitler and Stalin and Nixon has not been negligible.

Yet for practical purposes all this is largely academic, missing the main point: individual aggression, based on genetic and/or learning factors (frustrations, anger, hate, vindictiveness) is not the most important issue at all; *social destruction* is. Not that there is any question that such individual aggressive tendencies exist in abundance, and are used and redirected by those in power who primarily determine social behavior, and who frequently enough are profoundly hostile and aggressive themselves. But social destruction as we have seen is above all due to obedience to some authority, institution, or ideal. Thus it is most often committed without any personal feelings of hate, anger, or aggression against the victim at all. One only does one's "duty."

For whatever the speculations about man's "basic nature," we know three facts:

(1) Auschwitz.

(2) We are easily manipulated, for worse and even for better.

(3) We often become quickly brutalized, given an encouraging situation.

Compelling examples of the latter are man's conduct in war, Professor Zimbardo's prison experiment at Stanford, and the following:

> In his widely acclaimed novel, *Lord of the Flies,* Golding portrays the violent and savage relationships that develop among a group of English schoolboys shipwrecked on an isolated island. Forced to manage for themselves in order to survive, the boys disagree fiercely. The initial dominance hierarchy is overthrown, and violence results. One boy is killed, and when the group is finally rescued, the original leader is being hunted with the cries: "Kill the beast! Cut his throat!

Spill his blood!" *Lord of the Flies,* of course, is fiction. Its validity as a statement of human nature might be dismissed, were it not for the dramatic consequences that resulted from an effort to film the novel. The careful attempt to create Golding's story was almost too authentic.

The director of the film, Peter Brook:

Many of their off-screen relationships completely paralleled the story, and one of our main problems was to encourage them to be uninhibited within the shots but disciplined in between them. . . . My experience showed me that the only falsification in Golding's fable is the length of time the descent to savagery takes. His action takes about three months. I believe that if the cork of continued adult presence were removed from the bottle, the complete catastrophe could occur within a long weekend.[3]

So what must we conclude on the basis of the best evidence available?

With statistically insignificant and unrepresentative exceptions, humanity has demonstrated some innate propensity for destruction throughout the vast majority of history. That humanity's abundance of destruction is due to an innate tendency or learning is not 100% certain. One does not obtain certainty in science, history, or whatever. One merely makes the best conclusions that one can make, based on the available evidence. In this case, the evidence of history suggests that it is exceedingly likely that there is some innate propensity in humanity for destruction. . . .

There is no known or conceivable way in which destructiveness, if it were of socio-cultural origin, could have spread to so many dispersed and geographically isolated cultures as it has appeared in across the earth and throughout history. . . .

What is suggested here is not a teaching, training, or manipulation of people. Instead, the antecedent conditions, which will facilitate the inner realization within people, both rationally and intuitively, that humanity must begin acting in a socially responsible way—are the keys. . . .

The immediacy with which this "social sense" must be facilitated cannot be overemphasized. Careful evaluation of history shows that the failure of humanity to destroy itself has not been due to a lack of effort. Rather it has been largely due to inefficient methods for producing vast destruction. Modern weapons such as atomic warheads, germ warfare, and nerve gas are not inefficient methods of destruction. From history, it can be seen humanity can also act constructively. The time for constructive and socially responsible behavior is now, while it is still a possibility.[4]


### Appendix E    *The Criterion of Social Adjustment*

The most common answer given by those convicted of war crimes, i.e., "I only followed orders," was frequently only in part a self-serving and dishonest excuse. Often the accused believed that the responsibility had in fact not been theirs anymore. Like many others, Hoess bitterly complained that by committing suicide Himmler had failed to live up to his part of the bargain: had it not been he who ordered the exterminations? Had he not thereby assumed responsibility for them?

And when Captain Wirz, in charge of the 33,000 Union prisoners at the infamous Andersonville Camp, was about to be hanged (quite drunk from the whiskey he had just consumed), he called out: "I am being hanged for obeying them!" Jefferson Davis understood; shortly before his own death he tried to justify the conditions at Andersonville and described Wirz as a "martyr."

The psychologists Ullmann and Krasner in *A Psychological Approach to Abnormal Behavior*, ask if maladaptive behavior is a required characteristic of mental illness. They answer the question by stating that if such a requirement is not made, the way is open for total societies to be designated as sick. In line with this reasoning, how do they view the obedient Nazi concentration camp commander? They consider him *normal,* since he was "responding accurately and successfully [!] to his environment." (p. 15) Hoess would have agreed. The possibility that this environment was abnormal is either not seen as a relevant consideration, or the authors are afraid of becoming involved in the sticky implications of considering it so. The result is that the most important cause of destruction has thus either been misunderstood or avoided.

And what position must we take on the basis of the evidence we have seen?

First, countries, societies, cultures, authorities, institutions, and organizations do not exist independently of the people who constitute them. How could a society possibly be criminal and insane, however defined, but not the members without whom it would not exist? How could these members possibly be criminal and insane but not their society? And how could a systematically criminal and irrational society not produce systematically criminal and irrational individuals?

Secondly, concerning responsibility and guilt, societies, organizations, and other abstracts do not *behave*. Men do. I want to make this point clear:

—General Motors does not produce shoddy automobiles; its engineers and workers do.

—Science does not construct thermonuclear devices and poison gas; scientists do.

—The Republican Party did not elect Mr. Nixon; Republicans and other Americans did.

—The Church did not burn heretics at the stake; Christians did.

—Germany did not exterminate the Jews; Nazis and other Germans did.

—The Soviet Union did not crush the Czech "revolt" in 1968; Russian soldiers in Russian tanks did.

—America did not commit atrocities in Vietnam; Americans did.

Indeed they did all this in the name of their organization, their science, their party, their Church, their Nazism, their Communism, their Americanism. But it is *men* who burn, shoot, gas, and drop napalm. No country, society, institution, authority, or ideal ever killed anyone.

If this is not understood, we shall once again make the mistake with which this book is concerned and which Milgram described as "counteranthropomorphism," the elevation of institutions into values, and even more importantly the tendency to attribute an impersonal quality to forces which are essentially human in origin and maintenance. To express it differently, men obey authorities, institutions, and ideals, but in doing so they obey other men.

Appendix F    *An American and a German General: A comparison.*

General George Patton: "War is the supreme test of a man."

George S. Patton, Jr., grew up overprotected in near-isolation on an 1800-acre ranch with an opinionated father and an athletic and active mother.

At West Point he was as unpopular with his fellow cadets as he was popular with his instructors, whom he impressed by a punctilious obedience of rules.

From Charles Whiting's *Patton:*

> As a man, Patton was sometimes a fool, sometimes a neurotic, often a foul-mouthed bore and braggart. He could drive men into battle with the unnecessary vulgarity of his language and inspect their dead bodies later on the field of battle with apparently no remorse that he had caused, in part, their death. Yet at the same time he could weep unashamedly at the sight of wounded soldiers in hospitals and pray regularly to a God who had commanded "Thou shalt not kill."

Stiff-necked, arrogant, and boastful, his lack of social judgment was notorious, and his superiors, in particular Generals Marshall, Eisenhower, and Bradley, were always worried about keeping him in line. In a speech in England in 1944, for example, he concluded that "it is the evident destiny of the British and American people to rule the world." The impact of this declaration upon the suggested super-races' ally at the time, Russia, was not favorable.

Shortly after World War II, removed by Eisenhower from command of his beloved Third Army, and feeling useless without battles to fight, he died following a car accident on a German country road.

He would have much preferred to have spilled his blood and guts on some battlefield.

Field Marshal Gerd von Rundstedt: "Certainly we think earnestly of the dead, but we do not mourn."

Von Rundstedt's family belonged to the old Prussian nobility dating back to the 12th century. His ancestors would have been proud of him: cold, rigid, silent, functional, efficient, self-disciplined, hard-faced, loyal, computerized. In 1939 he surrounded the main Polish armies west of Warsaw; a year later in France he reached the Channel within eleven days; and in Russia he commanded the Southern Army Group, the most successful (it was to reach Stalingrad).

He despised the storm troopers, the Brown Shirts, whom he called "brown dirt"; refused to give the Nazi salute; and knew very well what Churchill meant when he spoke of the "warlike genius by which Corporal Schicklegruber so notably contributed to our victory." Without Hitler's interference he would have captured the British Army at Dunkirk—with not insignificant consequences.

Not that any of this made the slightest difference. Von Rundstedt, a proverbial Prussian officer with a proverbial Prussian sense of "honor," prided himself on being totally detached from politics. This allowed him:

(1) To do Hitler's bidding to the end.

(2) To preside over the Court of Honor expelling from the officer corps those involved in the 20th of July assassination attempt (who were thereafter turned over to the People's Court, which, among other things, ordered a fellow field marshal strangled to death on a meathook).

(3) To issue an order during the mammoth massacre of 33,000 Jewish civilians at Babi Yar, a ravine near Kiev, forbidding soldiers to watch or photograph the executions. In the field marshal's sense of priorities mass murder was less objectionable than voyeurism and amateur photography.

The Allies naturally considered him to have done nothing criminal, and he retired with a comfortable pension and died peacefully in his bed.

The picture of the Kaiser still hung on his wall.

Patton and von Rundstedt—two militarily highly competent generals who faced each other in France but who would have agreed, one more emotionally and the other more intellectually, that war is the perfect act of violence, "the great drama of mankind, the supreme murder mystery, composed in music of pure action, abstract death, and the whole orchestra of economics, science, culture and human societies."

Appendix G    *The Air War and the Atomic Bomb: A Judgment*

The air war deserves careful evaluation. Numerical confusion, moral ambivalence, and in general sloppy and prejudicial thinking have resulted in sentimental generalizations and both unjustified accusations and unadmitted guilt.

To begin with, it is specifically the destruction of Dresden to which I object. Filled with refugees from the East, most of whom suffocated or burned to death, Dresden was of no military importance, and Marshal Konev's armies were already within 70 miles. Churchill, too, had his misgivings; following the virtual death of the city after the raids of February 13 and 14, 1945, with estimates of the number of persons killed starting at 135,000, he wrote to his Chiefs of Staff: "It seems to me that the moment has come when the question of bombing German cities simply for the sake of increasing the terror should be reviewed. . . . I feel the need for more precise concentration upon military objectives . . . rather than on mere acts of terror and wanton destruction, however impressive."[1]

The Chiefs of Staff, in particular Air Marshal Portal of the Royal Air Force, forced the Prime Minister to withdraw this minute.[2]

Nor did Stalin need to be impressed, as another argument goes: the great firebombing of Tokyo was a few weeks away (97,000 killed, 125,000 wounded); Alamogordo a few months.

As for the air war in general, it now seems that it would have been much more productive to attack ball-bearing plants and oil refineries instead of civilians. Perhaps this was unknown to the Allies at the time; given the more recent bombing of Vietnam this appears ever more unlikely. (General Shoup: "In fact, it became increasingly clear that the United States bombing effort in both North and South Vietnam has been one of the most wasteful and expensive hoaxes ever to be put over on the American people.")

Such priorities were not unknown to the most directly affected German leader, Albert Speer, Minister of Armaments and Munitions:

> The war could largely have been decided in 1943 if instead of vast but pointless bombing the planes had concentrated on the centers of armament production.[3]

And:

> In June 1946 the General Staff of the RAF asked me what would have been the results of concerted attacks on the ballbearing industry. I replied: Armaments production would have been crucially weakened after two months and after four months would have been brought completely to a standstill.[4]

Quite different considerations apply to Hiroshima. Truman has been indicted by many for his decision to drop the atomic bomb, and while some object to the introduction of a new type of weapon, most take issue with its immediate destructive effects. Concerning the latter reasoning, material facts are as follows:

(1) Japanese military strength as of 18 June 1945 stood at 4,615,000 men, including 1,415,000 in Japan proper.[5]

(2) Japanese fighting morale not only remained high but often improved as the battles approached the homeland, despite the continuous setbacks. Had the Emperor decreed to fight on, there is little doubt that his subjects would have complied.

(3) Japanese psychology at the time is particular food for thought: On Iwo Jima, an eight-square-mile island of volcanic ash whose only importance lay in its airfield, three Marine Corps divisions fought 26 days against about 23,000 Japanese; the Americans suffered 20,000 casualties. Of the Japanese garrison one percent were taken prisoner. Counterattacking on Okinawa on April 6 and 7, their force included 350 kamikaze planes and the *Yamato,* the world's largest battleship—with only enough fuel for a one-way trip. 110,000 Japanese died on the island.

(4) Having lived in Japan a year and a half, I have some first-hand impressions of the likely cost of an invasion of the mainland. And with estimates of casualties running into millions, Truman had no illusions of which was the lesser evil:

"The final decision of where and when to use the atomic bomb was up to me. Let there be no mistake about it. I regarded the bomb as a military weapon and never had any doubt that it should be used. The top military advisors to the President recommended its use, and when I talked to Churchill he unhesitatingly told me he favored the use of the atomic bomb if it might end the war."[6]

(5) Careful estimates indicate that about 120,000 people were killed or died of their injuries in Hiroshima and Nagasaki. Whether the bombing of Nagasaki was militarily justified is questionable. But Hiroshima had served its purpose: Four days later the Japanese government announced its readiness to surrender.

(6) "I think that the dropping of the atomic bomb was unfortunate but it was an event that occurred in the midst of war. For the people of Hiroshima it was a pitiful thing, but I believe it could not be helped."— Emperor Hirohito, October 1975.

Appendix H    *The Psychology of the Victim: A Statement of the Problem.*

At Auschwitz, two thousand SS guards murdered about two million victims, mostly Jews.

In Russia, the three thousand SS members of the four *Einsatzgruppen,* Heydrich's mobile extermination units, hunted down and killed close to another million.

Does this mean that the victims went like sheep to their slaughter? And how would we know the answer? This book is primarily concerned with the psychology of the murderer and the "bystander"; but what about the psychology of the victim? Is it perhaps the reverse side of the coin? Was his behavior, in its own way, still due to his obedience to his Holy Cows—as well as possibly the enemy's? It is not enough to weep at the Israeli lullaby, "The grass is green where your father fell." The question is why and how he fell. And what, if anything, he could have done about it. There are, after all, few alternatives not preferable to the gas chamber or the mass grave.

We know that there were those who collaborated and those who gave up without a fight, physical or mental. Those who did not even know what happened to them, or why. And those who resisted.

A prisoner by the name of Frank, or Franke, a man of about forty:

> He spoke little, but looked kindly at everyone. He had thin, wavy, fair hair above a smooth forehead, large blue eyes, rosy cheeks, an effeminate mouth, and a rather small round chin. . . . Untiringly he swept the cell, and the corridor, fetched water, and made himself useful to everybody. But when the SS guards discovered that he never raised his arm and refused to say "Heil Hitler!" they gave him a week of solitary confinement in the "dark cell."
>
> When he returned his eyes were blood-shot.
>
> "Be sensible," his comrades said to him. "What does this bit of 'Heil Hitler' matter! Do as we do, with your tongue in your cheek."
>
> He shook his head. The next day he was found out again. This time he spent a fortnight in the dark cell. We

could scarcely recognize him when he came out. But he did not raise his arm to salute.

Now fat Zimmermann took it on himself to teach him. Accompanied by five SS men, Franke was led down to the little courtyard.

"Up with your arm. Up with your arm!"

The Commander looked on.

"Up with your arm!"

They fell on him. He rolled down into the ice-covered pools. "Arm up! Heil Hitler! Get a move on!"

This went on until he lay there unconscious. His blood froze on the ground.

We implored him. In vain. His face became set, with a childish obstinate expression. He would not salute. We felt desperate. Now he was separated from us and put into the cells with the habitual criminals. He was given the same uniform as they. Day after day he had to run along with the latrine boxes. His hands were bloody from the strain. He spent his life between arrest, blows and latrine duty.

We nodded kindly to him when we saw him. We whispered to him. We stretched our arms to show him the salute. The SS men had bets on him. After many weeks he joined us again.

On entering the corridor, he met an SS man. His right arm rose awkwardly. His hand, crusted with blood, stretched out. He whispered:

"Heil Hitler."[1]

So how does one fight?
And how does one survive?
And at what cost?
Is the old prisoner right, telling the new arrivals:

We are all brothers and we are all suffering the same fate. The same smoke floats over our heads. Help one another. It is the only way to survive.[2]

Or is the anonymous inmate right:

Listen to me, boy. Don't forget that you're in a concentration camp. Here, every man has to fight for himself and not think of anyone else. Even of his father. Here, there are no fathers, no brothers, no friends. Everyone lives and dies for himself alone.[2]

Or is Primo Levi right in *Survival in Auschwitz:*

There comes to light the existence of two particularly well differentiated categories among men—the saved and the drowned. Other pairs of opposites (the good and the bad, the wise and the foolish, the cowards and the courageous, the unlucky and the fortunate) are considerably less distinct, they seem less essential, and above all they allow for more numerous and complex intermediary gradations . . . To sink is the easiest of matters; it is enough to carry out all the orders one receives, to eat only the ration, to observe the discipline of the work and the camp. Experience showed that only exceptionally could one survive more than three months in this way. All the mussulmans who finished in the gas chambers have the same story, or more exactly, have no story; they followed the slope down to the bottom, like streams that run down to the sea. On their entry into the camp, through basic incapacity, or by misfortune, or through some banal incident, they are overcome before they can adapt themselves; they are beaten by time, they do not begin to learn German, to disentangle the infernal knot of laws and prohibitions until their body is already in decay, and nothing can save them from selections or from death by exhaustion. Their life is short, but their number is endless; they the *Muselmanner,* the drowned, form the backbone of the camp, an anonymous mass continually renewed and always identical, of non-men who march and labour in silence, the divine spark dead within them, already too empty to really suffer. One hesitates to call them living: one hesitates to call their death death, in the face of which they have no fear, as they are too tired to understand. . . With the mussulmans, the men in decay, it is not even worth speaking, because one knows already that they will complain and will speak about what they used to eat at home . . . Survival without renunciation of any part of one's own moral world—apart from powerful and direct interventions by fortune—was conceded only to very few superior individuals, made of the stuff martyrs and saints . . .

Theft in Buna, punished by the civil direction, is authorized and encouraged by the SS; theft in camp, severely repressed by the SS, is considered by the civilians as a normal exchange operation; theft among [prisoners] is generally punished, but the punishment strikes the thief and the victim with equal gravity . . . We now invite the reader to contemplate the possible meaning in the Lager of the words "good" and "evil," "just" and "unjust"; let everybody judge, on the basis of the picture we have outlined and of the examples given above, how much of our ordinary moral world could survive on this side of the barbed wire.

Or is Dr. Lingens-Reiner right, describing a fellow Auschwitz prisoner:

Ena Weiss, our Chief Doctor—one of the most intelligent, gifted and eminent Jewish women in the camp—once defined her attitude thus, in sarcastic rejection of fulsome flattery and at the same time with brutal frankness: "How did I keep alive in Auschwitz? My principle is: myself first, second and third. Then nothing. Then myself again—and then all the others." This formula expressed the only principle which was possible for Jews who intended—almost insanely intended—to survive Auschwitz. Yet, because this woman had the icy wisdom and strength to accept the principle, she kept for herself a position in which she could do something for the Jews. Hardly anybody else in the camp did as much for them and saved so many lives as she did.

Is this what Bettelheim means when he states that under such extraordinary circumstances man cannot go on with business as usual, but must radically reevaluate all of what he has done, believed in, stood for? And what are we to make of the historian Dawidowicz' moral judgment about Jewish behavior during the holocaust: "All are guilty, or perhaps more truly, all are innocent and holy." What of the claim that the mass murder of the Jews by the Nazis was *qualitatively* different from other mass murders? And what of the question Wiesenthal raises in *The Sunflower?* A young Jew is taken from a death camp to an Army hospital where a blind and dying SS soldier confesses to him his part in the burning alive of an entire village of Jews—begging for this Jew's absolution. From the book's jacket:

Having listened to the Nazi's story for several hours—
torn between horror and compassion for the dying
man—the Jew finally walks out of the room without
speaking. Was his action right? or moral? That
challenging question forms the basis for the fascinating
symposium of responses that follows Wiesenthal's
story, including the opinions of Herman Wouk, Rene
Cassin, Hans Habe, Jacob Kaplan, Kurt von
Schuschnigg, Herbert Marcuse, and Terence Prittie, to
mention only a few . . .

But is it a meaningful question at all? What is its
relevance? Is it not an outrage for you or me or anyone to
claim the "right" to "forgive," whatever that may mean?
Should the question not be the opposite: Why has so much
crime been committed by so many and paid for by so few?

What are the facts? What should our ethical criteria be,
and what do we pretend they are? Where lies the truth?

Very unfortunately, almost all attempts to explain Nazi
victims' behavior have been psychoanalytically oriented,
as well as confined to life in the camps, where the possibility of resistance was drastically reduced. A definite *scientific* study of the psychology of the victim has yet to be
written. It is the least the survivors can do for the
murdered: for those who resisted, and for those who
should have.[3]

During the terrible years of Yezhovshchina I spent
seventeen months in the prison queues in Leningrad.
One day someone recognized me. Then a woman with
lips blue with cold who was standing behind me, and of
course had never heard of my name, came out of the
numbness which affected us all and whispered in my
ear—(we all spoke in whispers there): "Can you describe
this?" I said, "I can!"
  Then something resembling a smile slipped over what
had once been her face.—Anna Akhmatova, *Requiem*

Appendix I    *An SS Mass Execution: An Eyewitness Account.*

A comparatively minor mass execution of five thousand Jews was observed by the manager of a German construction firm in the occupied Ukraine. It was October 5, 1942.

Sworn affidavit by Hermann Friedrich Graebe, read to the Nuremberg Court by the Chief British Prosecutor, Sir Hartley Shawcross, on July 27, 1946:

> Without screaming or weeping the people undressed, stood around in family groups, kissed each other, said farewells, and waited for a sign from another SS man, who stood near the pit, also with a whip in his hand. During the 15 minutes that I stood near I heard no complaint or plea for mercy. I watched a family of about 8 persons, a man and a woman both about 50 with their children of about 1, 8 and 10, and 2 grown-up daughters about 20–24. An old woman with snow-white hair was holding the 1-year-old child in her arms and singing to it and tickling it. The child was cooing with delight. The couple were looking on with tears in their eyes. The father was holding the hand of a boy about 10 years old and speaking to him softly; the boy was fighting his tears. The father pointed to the sky, stroked his head and seemed to explain something to him. At that moment the SS man at the pit shouted something to his comrade. The latter counted off about 20 persons and instructed them to go behind the earth mound. Among them was the family which I have mentioned. I well remember a girl, slim and with black hair who, as she passed close to me, pointed to herself and said, "23." I walked around the mound and found myself confronted by a tremendous grave. People were closely wedged together and lying on top of each other so that only their heads were visible. Nearly all had blood running over their shoulders from their heads. Some of the people shot were still moving. Some were lifting their arms and turning their heads to show that they were still alive. The pit was already two-thirds full. I estimated that it contained already about 1,000 people. I looked for the man who did the shooting. He was an SS man, who sat at the edge of the narrow end of the pit, his feet dangling into

the pit. He had a tommy gun on his knees and was smoking a cigarette. The people, completely naked, went down some steps which were cut in the clay wall of the pit and clambered over the heads of the people lying there, to the place which the SS man directed them. Then I heard a series of shots. I looked into the pit and saw that the bodies were twitching or the heads lying motionless on top of the bodies which lay before them. Blood was running away from their necks.

## Appendix J   *My Lai. An Eyewitness Account.*

From an interview with Mike Wallace of CBS News *(The New York Times,* November 25, 1969): . . .

A: We moved into the village, and we started searching up the village and gathering people and running through the center of the village.

Q: How many people did you round up?

A: Well, there was about forty, fifty people that we gathered in the center of the village. And we placed them in there, and it was like a little island, right there in the center of the village, I'd say.
   . . . And . . .

Q: What kind of people—men, women, children?

A: Men, women, children.

Q: Babies?

A: Babies. And we huddled them up. We made them squat down and Lieutenant Calley came over and said, "You know what to do with them, don't you?" And I said yes. So I took it for granted that he just wanted us to watch them. And he left, and he came back about ten or fifteen minutes later and said, "How come you ain't killed them yet?" And I told him that I didn't think you wanted us to kill them, that you just wanted us to guard them. He said, "No, I want them dead." So—

Q: He told this to all of you, or to you particularly?

A: Well, I was facing him. So, but the other three, four guys heard it and so he stepped back about ten, fifteen feet,and he started shooting them. And he told me to start shooting. So I started shooting, I poured about four clips into the group.

Q: You fired four clips from your . . .

A: M-16.

Q: And that's about how many clips—I mean how many—

A: I carried seventeen rounds to each clip.

Q: So you fired something like sixty-seven shots?

A: Right.

Q: And you killed how many? At that time?

A: Well, I fired them automatic, so you can't—you just spray the area on them and so you can't know how many you killed, 'cause they were going fast. So I might have killed ten or fifteen of them.

Q: Men, women, and children?

A: Men, women, and children.

Q: And babies?

A: And babies.

. . .

A: [then] somebody told us to switch off to single shot so that we could save ammo. So we switched off to single shot, and shot a few more rounds . . .

Q: Why did you do it?

A: Why did I do it? Because I felt like I was ordered to do it, and it seemed like that, at the time I felt like I was doing the right thing, because, like I said, I lost buddies. I lost a damn good buddy, Bobby Wilson, and it was on my conscience. So, after I done it, I felt good, but later on that day, it was getting to me.

Q: You're married?

A: Right.

Q: Children?

A: Two.

Q: How old?

A: The boy is two and a half, and the little girl is a year and a half.

Q: Obviously, the question comes to my mind . . . the father of two little kids like that . . . how can he shoot babies?

A: I didn't have the little girl. I just had the little boy at the time.

Q: Uh-huh . . . How do you shoot babies?

A: I don't know. It's just one of those things.

Q: How many people would you imagine were killed that day?

A:    I'd say about three hundred and seventy.

Q:    How do you arrive at the figure?

A:    Just looking.

Q:    You say you think that many people, and you yourself were responsible for how many?

A:    I couldn't say.

Q:    Twenty-five? Fifty?

A:    I couldn't say. Just too many.

Q:    And how many men did the actual shooting?

A:    Well, I really couldn't say that either. There was other . . . there was another platoon in there, and . . . but I just couldn't say how many.

Q:    But these civilians were lined up and shot? They weren't killed by crossfire?

A:    They weren't lined up . . . They [were] just pushed in a ravine, or just sitting, squatting . . . and shot.

Q:    What did these civilians—particularly the women and children, the old men—what did they do? What did they say to you?

A:    They weren't much saying to them. They [were] just being pushed and they were doing what they was told to do.

Q:    They weren't begging, or saying, "No. . . no," or . . .

A:    Right. They were begging and saying, "No, no." And the mothers was hugging their children, and . . . but they kept right on firing. Well, we kept right on firing. They was waving their arms and begging. . . .

The soldier was not brought to trial for his role at My Lai as he was no longer under military jurisdiction at the time the massacre came to public attention.

From *Newsweek,* May 10, 1976:

Marriage planned: William L. Calley, Jr., 32, the former Army lieutenant who served 40 months in confinement as the only defendant convicted for a role in the My Lai massacre of South Vietnamese civilians in 1968, and Martha Penelope (Penny) Vick, 29, a buyer for her family's jewelry store in Columbus, Ga. . . . scheduled for May 15 at a Methodist church in Columbus.

## Appendix K    *A Summary of the Book in Twenty-six Quotes*

*"Kuhn is out of his senses. Does he not see Beppo the Greek in the bunk next to him, Beppo who is twenty years old and is going to the gas chamber the day after tomorrow and knows it and lies there looking fixedly at the light without saying anything and without even thinking any more? Can Kuhn fail to realize that next time it will be his turn? Does Kuhn not understand that what has happened today is an abomination, which no propitiatory prayer, no pardon, no expiation by the guilty, which nothing at all in the power of man can ever clean again?"*

*Primo Levi,* Survival in Auschwitz

*"We rely on the sane people of the world to preserve it from barbarism, madness, destruction. And now it begins to dawn on us that it is precisely the* sane *ones who are the most dangerous . . . who can without qualm and without nausea aim the missiles and press the buttons that will initiate the great festival of destruction that they, the* sane ones, *have prepared."*

*Judd Marmor*

*Freud's biographer, Ernest Jones, once told him the story of a surgeon who said that if he ever reached the Eternal Throne he would come armed with a cancerous bone and ask the Lord what he had to say for himself.*

*Freud remarked that if he were to find himself in a similar situation his chief reproach would be that he had not been given a better brain.*

*I would ask the Almighty what he had to say about Auschwitz.*

*"Crime, like disease, is not interesting: it is something to be done away with by general consent, and that is all about it. It is what men do at their best, and what normal men and women find they must and will do in spite of their intentions, that really concerns us."*

*George Bernard Shaw,* Preface to Saint Joan, *1923*

*"Yet all who played a role in the drama, even Marat, believed themselves motivated by patriotic or altruistic impulses. All in consequence were able to value their good intentions more highly than human life, for there is no crime, no murder, no massacre that cannot be justified, provided it be committed in the name of some ideal."*

*Stanley Loomis,* Paris in the Terror

*"There is something honest about sadistic, personal cruelty compared, say, with the remarkable Requirement that the Spaniards read to the Indians in order to justify the persecution that was soon to follow. The Requirement was read aloud at them in such a way that no Indian had a chance to reply before the onslaught of the slavers and the killers. And sometimes it was read with no Indians present, to trees, to deserted villages, and even to the open sea before coming into port. Only a longheld, deep institutional commitment could cause men to believe in such a sham."*

*Philip Hallie,* Justification and Rebellion

*"Hitler had reckoned in advance on a certain resistance from the middle classes. It was literally impossible to build a state relying only on his uniformed rowdies. [But had he] ever been in a position to write his memoirs he would have reminded all those Germans who allegedly strove to prevent "the worst" from happening that in building up his power the inwardly hesitant middle classes had been, with their ability and sense of duty, the most valuable of all his collaborators."*

*Hermann Eich,* The Unloved Germans

*"There are great advantages in knowing right from wrong with inexorable exactitude. Whole clumps of moral life are immediately removed from your concern. Jews stink, the Irish are lushes, Greeks cheat, Italians are sex fiends, and Arabs are worse. This is a comfortable world, just like in the silents, when the good guys wore big, white Stetsons and the bad guys wore big, black ones."*

*Charles McCabe*

*"The norms of sportsmanlike conduct on which, I suppose, good hunters pride themselves strike me as highly hypocritical; the minimum conditions for 'fair combat,' it seems to me, would be to allow the game free choices of participation and parity of weapon— conditions [as] noticeably lacking in the gentlemanly sport of hunting as they are in sanctioned massacres."*

*Herbert Kelman*

*"Our troubles emanate not from biological idiots but from social ones; and social idiots are produced by society, not by genes. It is, therefore, social and not biological therapy that is indicated."*

*Ashley Montagu*

*"Cruelty    and    compassion    come    with    the chromosomes;*
*All men are merciful and all are murderers.*
*Doting on dogs, they build their Dachaus;*
*Fire whole cities and fondle the orphans;*
*Are loud against lynching, but all for Oakridge;*
*Full of future philanthropy, but today the NKVD.*
*Whom shall we persecute, for whom feel pity?*
*It is all a matter of the moment's mores,*
*Of words on wood pulp, of radios roaring,*
*Of Communist kindergartens and first communions.*
*Only in the knowledge of his own Essence*
*Has any man ceased to be many monkeys."*

*Aldous Huxley*

*"The solution to the puzzle is this; only in logic are contradictions unable to coexist, in feelings they quite happily continue alongside each other."*

*Sigmund Freud*

*"People generally assume that the preservation or success of a society depends on a certain amount of dirty work—acts which most 'good people' prefer not to think about too closely, including internal repression. Society is organized so that they are not forced to do so. The dirty work, such as repressing people declared to be enemies of the state, is done by relatively small corps of men who are not shocked by killing or*

*brutality and may even enjoy it. What country can claim to be without such men? If they are organized and sanctioned by the state and if most people regard the work as necessary or at least excusable (insofar as they think about it at all), then who is to stop the dirty work? Since the brutality is described to the public only in attractive metaphors or in bureaucratic euphemisms, the good people are allowed both to keep their consciences clean and to participate vicariously in the scapegoating. They see any 'excesses' as necessary responses forced on a reluctant staff by the perfidy of the victims."*

E.C. Hughes

*"  'In the end,' says the Grand Inquisitor in Dostoevski's parable, 'in the end they will lay their freedom at our feet and say to us, "make us your slaves, but feed us . . . " for nothing,' the Inquisitor insists, 'has ever been more insupportable for a man or human society than freedom.' "*

*from* The Brothers Karamazov

*"Disobedience, in the eyes of anyone who has read history, is man's original virtue."*

Oscar Wilde

*"Two things are infinite, the universe and human stupidity . . . and I am not yet sure about the universe."*

Albert Einstein

*"Progress of science and technology without progress of conscience leads only to the result that slaves are not driven with ropes around their necks, but are shipped in modern sealed cars; and the fascist kills not with a simple club, but with a late- model submachine gun or with Cyclone B gas."*

A. Kuznetsov

*"To the already established arsenals of thermonuclear weapons for mega-murder— instantaneous obliteration of populations by the millions—there are now being elaborated weapons systems for wilful deterioration of climate or piercing and destroying our planet's protective ozone shield.*

*"The prime mover behind this development is no anonymous, self-generating force. It is nothing but the competition between some great powers who legitimize the production and consequently also the use of ever more cruel weapons . . . As political motivations for this massive production of military means of destruction is offered that it serves to protect 'national security.' But it does not do so, anywhere. It only functions for unsettling any security balance that might be achieved. It is nothing but a gigantic miscalculation. . . . In my book I have not hesitated to characterize the gaming for war-fighting capabilities a 'terminal psychosis.' It is really, playing with the security, yes, possibly the very existence of our world."*

Alva Myrdal

*"It was not sheer hypocrisy when the rank-and-file Nazis declared themselves not guilty of all the enormities they had committed. They considered themselves cheated and maligned when made to shoulder responsibility for obeying orders. Had they not joined the Nazi movement to be free from responsibility?"*

Eric Hoffer

*"Why? Why did we walk like meek sheep to the slaughterhouse? Why did we not fight back? . . . I know why. Because we had faith in humanity. Because we did not really think that human beings were capable of committing such crimes."*

Gerda Klein, All But My Life

*"The wild grasses rustle over Babi Yar.*
*The trees look ominous,*

                                        *like judges.*
*Here all things scream silently*

                        *and, baring my head,*
*Slowly I feel myself turning gray."*

Yevgeny Yevtushenko, Babi Yar

*"Agony, agony, dream, ferment and dream.*
*This is the world, my friend, agony, agony.*
*The corpses decompose under the clock of the cities.*
*War passes weeping with a million grey rats,*

*the rich give to their mistresses*
*small illuminated moribunds,*
*and Life is not noble, nor good, nor sacred.''*
           *Federico Garcia Lorca,* Ode to Walt Whitman


*''Then he began to tell me about what it was like to be*
*a press correspondent under Hitler; it was a quasi-*
*military position and all news was censored from*
*above. The press corps knew plenty of things which*
*were kept from the general public and they deliberately*
*concealed them. They knew about death camps and*
*deportations. They knew and they still cranked out*
*propaganda.*

   *'But how could you* do *it?' I shouted.*
   *'How could I* not *do it?'*
   *'You could have left Germany, you could have joined*
*the Resistance, you could have done* something*!'*
   *'But I was not a hero, and I didn't want to be a*
*refugee. Journalism was my profession.'*
   *'So what!'*
   *'All I am saying is that most people are not heroes,*
*and most people are not honest. I don't say I'm good or*
*admirable. All I am saying is that I am like most*
*people.'*
   *'But* why?*' I whined.*
   *'Because I am,' he said. 'No reason.' ''*
           *Erica Jong,* Fear of Flying


*''More normal, at any rate, than I am after having*
*examined him.''*
   *One of the psychiatrists who declared Eichmann nor-*
*mal*

*''Piety and conformity to them that like,*
*Peace, obesity, allegiance, to them that like . . .*
*I am he who walks the States with a barb'd tongue,*
   *questioning everyone I meet,*
*Who are you that wanted only to be told*
   *what you knew before?*
*Who are you that wanted only a book*
   *to join you in your nonsense?''*
           *Walt Whitman,* By Blue Ontario's Shore

> *The murdered's clothes and other things found at Auschwitz (368,000 men's suits, 836,000 women's coats and dresses, large quantities of children's clothes, seven tons of hair) would have filled five hundred and thirty-six freight cars, a train four kilometers long.*

## Notes to Chapter 1

[1] Rudolf Hoess, *Commandant of Auschwitz*, p. 181.

[2] Gustave M. Gilbert, *Nuremberg Diary*, p. 229. Compare Appendix G, "The Psychology of the Victim."

[3] William Shirer, *The Rise and Fall of the Third Reich*, pp. 1,263–1,264.

[4] *International Military Tribunal*, Document 3868-PS, 33: 275–276.

[5] Lucy Dawidowicz, *The War against the Jews, 1933°1945*, p. 149.

[6] *Ibid.*, p. 403. Compare Appendix B for additional statistics on casualties.

[7] A major purpose of this book is to redefine certain terms. An understanding of the following traditional meanings is therefore essential: *Crime:* a violation of a law; *Abnormality:* for our purposes sadism, psychosis, or insanity; *Sadism*: the preference for obtaining sexual gratification through infliction of pain upon another; *Psychosis*: a severe impairment of a person's ability to think and feel appropriately, as in the schizophrenias—essentially a clinical term; *Insanity*: an individual's incapacity to understand what he does, or if it is wrong—essentially a legal term. For a more detailed definition of these terms, see Appendix A.

[8] Gustave M. Gilbert, *The Psychology of Dictatorship*, p. 258.

[9] Alan Wykes, *Himmler*, p. 21.

[10] Nazi ministers.

[11] Douglas Kelley, *22 Cells in Nuremberg*, p. 171.

[12] One example: "Inmate Max Kasner, detailed to remove corpses in Auschwitz, was ordered into the courtyard of a building: 'On the left side lay about 70 dead women. Specially selected beautiful individuals. Beautiful still in death,' he states. 'The breasts of the dead had been cut off, and from soft parts, such as the thighs, the flesh was cut out with long deep cuts. The ground slanted, and the sewer was stopped up with blood. We waded in blood far above the ankles' " (Hoehne, *The Order of the Death's Head: The Story of Hitler's SS*, p. 349).

[13] *Frankfurter Allgemeine Zeitung*, March 3, 1964.

## Notes to Chapter 2

[1] All quotes, unless otherwise noted, are taken from Milgram's book *Obedience to Authority*. Additional data concerning the experiments are listed in

Appendix C, and include a discussion of methodological and ethical criticisms raised.

² A common psychological method used to study learning consists in learning to associate one word with another.

## Notes to Chapter 3

¹ Gustave M. Gilbert, *The Psychology of Dictatorship,* p. 117.

² Walter Kaufmann, *The Faith of a Heretic,* p. 225.

³ Rattray Taylor, *Sex in History,* p. 22.

⁴ Hugh Trevor-Roper, *The Last Days of Hitler,* pp. 20, 21.

⁵ Walter Kaufmann, *The Faith of a Heretic,* pp. 235, 237, 266.

⁶ Nicholas Gage, [author of] *The Mafia Is Not an Equal Opportunity Employer.*

⁷ Merle Miller, *Plain Speaking,* pp. 304, 287.

⁸ Alan Clark, *The Donkeys,* p. 156.

⁹ Brigadier General Sir J. E. Edmonds, the official historian (Liddell Hart files). Quoted in Alan Clark's *The Donkeys,* p. 11.

¹⁰ There are many others. Almost half of the nearly 3,000 would-be lawyers who took the statewide bar examination in February 1975 in California failed the section on professional ethics. There are also many overlaps and interactions such as the one described, some years ago, as the "military intellectual"—men like Kahn, Hitch, and Kissinger who move freely through the corridors of the Pentagon and the State Department, rather as the Jesuits through the courts of Madrid and Vienna three centuries ago.

¹¹ For a comparison of an American and a Nazi general, see Appendix F.

¹² Alexander and Selesnick, *The History of Psychiatry.*

## Notes to Chapter 4

¹Robert J. Lifton, "Existential Evil," in Sanford and Comstock, *Sanctions for Evil,* p. 40. See Appendices I and J for eyewitness accounts of an SS mass execution and of My Lai.

²Even technically, My Lai was a mistake—Americans had meant to go into a different subhamlet where the Vietcong were really active.

³Compare Appendix C for details.

⁴Compare Grunfeld's *The Hitler File,* p. 309.

⁵Thus Paul West, reviewing Richard Friedenthal's *Goethe: His Life and Times.*

[6]The historian Richard Grunberger, in his excellent and scholarly study *The 12-Year Reich,* p. 277.

[7]Lucy Dawidowicz, in her historically very valuable but psychologically flawed *The War Against the Jews, 1933-45,* considers (in a footnote!) the motivation for Hitler's anti-Semitism to be "irrelevant" though elsewhere she concludes that without him the Final Solution would never have occurred.

[8]Richard Brown, *Historical Patterns of Violence in America,* in Graham and Gurr, *Violence in America,* p. 56.

[9]Gunnar Myrdal, *Critical Essays on Economics.*

[10]David Shoup, *The New American Militarism.*

[11]Merle Miller, *Plain Speaking,* p. 406.

## Notes to Chapter 5

[1]Gustave Gilbert, *The Psychology of Dictatorship,* p. 314. For a brief discussion of basic (instinctive) aggressiveness see Appendix F.

[2]This issue is one which most social scientists have either ignored or been incapable of handling. It is discussed in Appendix E.

[3]I do not, of course, mean to imply that a psychotic person who hears voices or thinks he is Napoleon should be considered normal. His problem is of an entirely different order—and usually harmless to society.

[4]Albert Ellis, *The American Sexual Tragedy.*

[5]Bob Woodward and Carl Bernstein, *The Final Days.*

[6]See Appendix B.

[7]Compare Alva Myrdal's profoundly important *The Game of Disarmament. How the United States and Russia Run the Arms Race.*

[8]Albert Speer, *Spandau: The Secret Diaries.*

[9]From a recent *Los Angeles Times* article.

[10]See Appendix G for a judgment of the air war and atomic bomb.

## Notes to Appendices

### A

[1]James Coleman, *Abnormal Psychology and Modern Life,* p. 396.

[2]Ibid., p. 16.

### B

[1]Lucy S. Dawidowicz, *The War Against the Jews,* p. 403. Other estimates: Gerald Reitlinger, *The Final Solution,* 5.72 million; Raul Hilberg, *The*

*Destruction of the European Jews,* 5.1 million; and the *Encyclopedia Judaica,* 5.82 million.

[2]"Ordinary homicides," that is to say, those on which criminal courts spend all their time and efforts, and which the average law-abiding citizen finds so appalling, are not included and are *by comparison* negligible, even in this violent country. In 1975, we recorded 20,000 homicides in the USA.

### D

[1]From *The Collected Papers of Sigmund Freud,* vol. 5, edited by Ernest Jones.

[2]"In Skinner's world the systematic use of positive reinforcement would induce humanity to behave in socially responsible ways merely because it would be rewarding for them to do so. The danger in this is that [were] the systems of reward altered to provide positive reinforcement for destructive behavior, then people would behave destructively because it would be rewarding for them to do so" (Travis Mead, *A Critique of Self- Actualization Theory and its Implications for Humanistic Psychotherapy and Society).*

[3]Jerry Wiggins, *The Psychology of Personality.*

[4]Travis Mead, *A Critique of Self-Actualization Theory and Its Implications for Humanistic Psychotherapy and Society.*

### G

[1]David Irving, *The Destruction of Dresden,* p. R250,251.

[2]Hans Dollinger, *The Decline and Fall of Nazi Germany and Imperial Japan,* p. 269.

[3]Albert Speer, *Inside the Third Reich,* p. 280.

[4]Ibid., p. 285.

[5]Hans Dollinger, *The Decline and Fall of Nazi Germany and Imperial Japan,* p. 321.

[6]Harry Truman, *Memoirs,* Vol. 1, p. 462.

### H

[1]Quoted in Grunfeld's first-rate *The Hitler File,* p. 169.

[2]From Elie Wiesel's *Night.* Compare also Terrence des Pres' uneven book, *The Survivor.*

[3]Compare *Fighting Auschwitz,* Józef Garlínski's detailed account of resistance in the camp and Jean-François Steiner's shattering *Treblinka.*

WITHDRAWN

Lee College Library.
Baytown, Texas